BITE-SIZED
SIZED
Blasphemy

BITE-SIZED
Blasphemy

Unapologetic Wisdom for
BUILDING A BUSINESS THAT ACTUALLY WORKS

SARAH KHAN

ALEMBIC
PRESS

Printed in the United States of America

Digital ISBN 979-8-9922520-1-9

Paperback ISBN 979-8-9922520-0-2

Published by Alembic Press

Hotchkiss, Colorado

www.alembicpress.com

To S and N.

May you always question the status quo, never shrink to fit into a box, and use your voices to speak the truths the world needs to hear. Even if it shuts its ears to you. Persevere.

CONTENTS

INTRODUCTION

We're here to challenge the bullshit status quo of entrepreneurship, uncover what it really takes to build a business that honors your life and vision, and maybe piss off a few gurus along the way.

If that sounds like music to your ears, congratulations —you're in the right place. Welcome to *Bite-Sized Blasphemy* where we're about to flip the script on everything you thought you knew about entrepreneurship.

I'm Sarah Khan, How Whisperer, Business Advisor, and BS-busting badass. For years, I've been the voice in the online business space calling out the emperor's new clothes. You know, those "sacred truths" we're all supposed to bow down to—hustle culture, overnight success stories, and the idea that if you're not miserable, you're not trying hard enough.

Well, I'm here to tell you it's all a bunch of nonsense.

After spending over two decades climbing the corporate ladder, I thought I had it all figured out. Then I jumped into entrepreneurship—and holy hell, was I in for a wake-up call. I quickly realized that the online business world was just as full of toxic expectations and unrealistic standards as the corporate world I'd left behind.

That's when I decided enough was enough. I started my podcast, *Business Blasphemy*, to challenge the norms, trends, and overall bullshit status quo of entrepreneurship. And now, I'm taking that mission one step further with this book.

So, what exactly are you holding in your hands right now? It's not your typical business advice book, that's for damn sure. This is a collection of 100 mini-essays, each one starting with a thought-provoking quote that'll make you question everything you've been told about running a business.

This book is divided into six sections, each designed to strip away the layers of bullshit that have been holding you back and help you build a business that actually works for you—not against you.

In Part 1, we're kicking things off with *All You Need Is To Be More Of You* where we'll cut through the crap and get you embracing your authentic, audacious self in business. Then in Part 2, we dive into *It May Not Be Sexy But...A Business Is A Business Is A Business*—because let's face it, building a solid foundation isn't glamorous, but it's damn important.

Next up is Part 3: *You Didn't Leave Your Nine To Five To Start A 24/7* where we'll tackle how to honor your capacity and set some real boundaries. Followed by Part 4, my personal favorite: *Unicorns, Pitchslaps, Get-Rich-Quick Schemes, And Other BS From The Business Trenches*, where we're calling bullshit on all the myths that are keeping you stuck.

In Part 5, the rubber meets the road in *This Entrepreneur Sh!t Is Not For The Faint Of Heart* where we get real about the challenges we all face. We'll wrap it up with Part 6: *There's No Such Thing As One-Size-Fits-All* where you'll learn to redefine success on your own terms.

Now, let me be crystal clear about what you can expect from this book. If you're looking for get-rich-quick schemes or promises of six figures in six days, you're in the wrong place. I don't do fairy tales, and I sure as hell don't do empty promises.

What you will get is real, practical advice based on years of experience—both my own and that of the countless entrepreneurs I've worked with. We're talking strategies for building a sustainable business, tips for setting boundaries that actually stick, and a healthy dose of reality checks when it comes to what it really takes to succeed as an entrepreneur.

And fair warning: I don't sugarcoat shit. If you're easily offended by colorful language or brutally honest opinions, you might want to buckle up. My style isn't for everyone, and that's okay. I'm not here to be your best friend or your cheerleader. I'm here to be the voice of reason in a space that's drowning in toxic positivity and magical thinking.

But here's the thing—beneath all the swearing and straight talk, there's a message of hope and empowerment. Because I truly believe that you can have success without all the fucking BS that they keep telling us is normal. You can build a business that honors you, your life, and your vision for what's possible.

This book is for the entrepreneurs who are tired of feeling like they're doing it wrong because they don't want to hustle 24/7. It's for the business owners who are sick of being told they need to "scale or fail." It's for anyone who's ever looked at the conventional wisdom in the online business space and thought, "There's got to be a better way."

And let me tell you something—there is a better way. But it starts with questioning everything. It starts with being willing to commit some serious business blasphemy.

So, how should you approach this book? Well, you could read it cover to cover, but that's not necessary. Each essay stands on its own, so feel free to jump around to whatever speaks to you in the moment. Having a mindset meltdown? Flip to section one. Feeling the pressure to scale when you're not ready? Section two's got your back.

Use this book as a reality check when you're feeling overwhelmed by the noise in the online business space. Use it as a permission slip to do things your way. And most importantly, use it as a reminder that you're not alone in feeling like there's something seriously wrong with the way we're told to do business.

Remember, your worth isn't determined by your follower count or your bank balance. Success doesn't mean shit if it doesn't make you happy, and you get to decide what success looks like for you. Whether that's a multi-million-dollar empire or a lean, mean solopreneur machine—it's all valid, as long as it aligns with your values and your vision.

So, are you ready to question everything you thought you knew about business? Are you prepared to ruffle some feathers and piss off a few gurus along the way? Good. Because it's time to strip away the bullshit, embrace your authenticity, and build a business that actually works for you.

Welcome Blasphemer. Let's do this.

Part 1

ALL YOU NEED IS TO BE MORE OF YOU

1

You don't need more courses. You don't need more qualifications. You don't need more skills. All you need is to be more of you.

Growing up in a small town, I was the only brown girl in my grade and I learned to become a master of disguise. I learned to change my language, my interests, even how I dressed—all to blend in, to survive. This chameleon act followed me into adulthood, shaping how I showed up in different spaces, from friend groups to corporate boardrooms.

But all that shape-shifting is exhausting. It's not just about wearing different hats; it's about becoming entirely different people. We're so busy trying to make people like us, accept us, embrace us, that we lose sight of who we really are.

I've realized that the restlessness, the stuckness, the constant fatigue—it's not because we lack skills or qualifications. It's because we've never acknowledged who we are and what we want. We're too busy chasing after the next course, the next certification, thinking it'll finally make us "enough."

But what if the key to confidence, to pursuing those big opportunities, isn't in adding more to your resume? What if it's found in peeling away those layers of false identities we've created for safety and acceptance and palatability?

It's time to dig deep and reconnect with your core self. When's the last time you actually sat down and said this is the real me this is the true me and felt it on a bone deep level? When you do that, when you embrace who you really are, everything becomes easier. Decisions become clearer. The exhaustion lifts. You start pursuing goals that truly matter to you, not just what you think you should want.

So stop trying to be more qualified. Stop being who you think people want you to be. Start being more you.

2

You do know what you want. You're often stuck or lacking clarity because you're worried about what someone else will think, or do. You're worried about how it'll look. You're worried about doing the "right" thing.

You're not actually stuck. You're scared. Scared of what? Of being judged, of failing, of succeeding, of standing out, of blending in—take your pick. But deep down, beneath all that fear and second-guessing, you already know what you want.

So why the hell aren't you going after it? Because somewhere along the line, we got it into our heads that there's a "right" way to do business, a "proper" path to success. Newsflash: that's all bullshit. It's just another way to keep us small, to keep us in line with what everyone else is doing.

But honey, you're not everyone else. You're you. Unique, messy, brilliant you. And your business should reflect that. Stop worrying about what @EntrepreneurBarbie is doing on Instagram or what some self-proclaimed guru says is the "correct" way to run your business.

Instead, get crystal fucking clear on what *you* want. Not what you think you should want, not what your coach told you to want, but what lights a fire in your soul. Then go after it with everything you've got. Will it be scary? Hell yes. Will some people judge you? Probably. But will it be worth it? Abso-fucking-lutely.

3

Audacious liberation is the bold act of freeing yourself from constraints, barriers, and limiting beliefs, in a way that might be seen as daring or unconventional, but it's all about challenging the status quo.

Audacity isn't about being reckless or overconfident. It's about having the courage to accomplish the extra-ordinary. For far too long, we've been told to sit down, be quiet, and conform. Then suddenly, as en-trepreneurs, we're told you have to stand out, you've got to do things to make yourself visible and be seen. But there's no bridge between "sit down and be quiet" and "stand up and make noise".

That's where audacious liberation comes in. It's about freeing yourself from the bullshit status quo that's been holding you back. It's about stepping into your power, not by force, but because staying small no longer feels comfortable.

When you embrace your audacity, you're clear on your worth, you're clear on what is on your heart, you have a clear focus and you get really tired of staying where you are. You stop giving a shit about what others think and start focusing on what truly matters to you. It's not about being pushy or bitchy—it's about leading with love, leading with compassion, inspiring others rather than browbeating them into submission.

Audacious liberation isn't just about mindset, though. It's about taking action. Because let's face it, all the positive thinking in the world won't mean jack if you're not willing to get off your ass and do something.

4

Your voice is your power.

Using your voice isn't just about being heard—it's about being understood, recognized, and remembered. It's not about shouting the loudest; it's about speaking clearly, more truthfully and with conviction.

When I talk about amplifying your voice, I'm not telling you to crank up the volume. I'm urging you to dig deep, to tap into that well of experience, expertise, and unique perspective that only you possess. It's about stripping away all the facades and all the masks that we have to wear, and embracing that inner voice that's uniquely yours.

Your voice is the thread that weaves through everything you do. It's in the content you create, the way you mentor others, the speeches you give. It's what makes people sit up and take notice, thinking, "Damn, that resonates." And when you use your voice to speak your truth, even when it's uncomfortable, well, that's leadership in action.

5

We often feel stuck without realizing that it's because of barriers we haven't even identified yet. Sure, we know the obvious ones—patriarchy, capitalism, gatekeeping, being a woman of color. These are real, valid, and tough to overcome. But I'm not talking about those. I'm talking about the invisible barriers—the internal ones. The beliefs we carry about whether we're good enough, not because someone told us we aren't, but because we don't believe we are.

We all walk around with these invisible barriers in our heads, these little stories we tell ourselves about who we are and what we're capable of. And let me tell you, most of the time, these stories are pure bullshit.

These internalized beliefs aren't always obvious. They're not the visible barriers like patriarchy or capitalism that we can point to and say, "That is what's holding me back." No, these are the sneaky ones, the invisible ones that have been with us so long we don't even notice them anymore.

Maybe it's the belief that you're not good enough. Maybe it's a limitation on what you think your potential is. Whatever the story, it's time to call bullshit on it.

These beliefs are like a lid on our own container of awesomeness. They're holding us back from truly stepping into our power, from embracing the fullness of who we are.

Sometimes it's not easy to spot them. These stories are often like a reflex because you've been holding onto them for so long. And you can't let go of what you don't know you're holding on to.

Take some time, sit down, really identify and challenge the stories and beliefs that you have floating around in your head that are no longer serving you. Name them out, speak them out, write them out—it doesn't matter how, just get them out of your head and into the world where you can see them for what they are. And then it's time to start burning them down.

6

Dragons do whatever the fuck they want, but they do it with purpose and they do it with intention, and that is how you lead in a way that is bold and genuine and deeply impactful.

When I say dragon, I'm not talking about fire-breathing monsters from fairy tales, but the essence of what they represent: unapologetic power, freedom, and purpose.

Being a dragon in business isn't about being destructive or selfish. It's about embracing that inner voice and those inner values. It's about having the courage to strip away all the facades and all the masks that we wear.

In the entrepreneurial world, we're often told to follow the rules, fit in, and not rock the boat. But you know what? That's not how you lead in a way that is bold and genuine and deeply impactful. That's how you become just another face in the crowd, another boring business owner spouting the same old crap.

So, I challenge you: stop seeking permission. Stop trying to fit into predefined molds or boxes. Embrace your authenticity, even when it feels uncomfortable.

Do whatever the fuck you want—but do it with purpose, do it with intention, and watch how deeply you can impact the world around you.

7

We have such an obsession with avoiding uncertainty. And yet, when you really look at life, nothing is certain and there is absolutely nothing outside of you that is within your control.

I've spent most of my life trying to control everything. In my career as a project manager, it was my job to anticipate risks, plan for contingencies, and keep everything running smoothly. But you know what? Life doesn't give a shit about your plans.

We're all walking around with this illusion that if we just prepare enough, if we just wait for the perfect moment, we can avoid uncertainty. But that's bullshit. Uncertainty is the only certainty we have.

I grew up in a culture where safety was paramount. "What will people say?" was our house motto. So I played it safe, waiting for the right moment, the perfect circumstances. And you know what happened? Nothing. Absolutely fucking nothing.

Because there is no right moment. There is no perfect time. There's just now, and what you choose to do with it. Yeah, it's scary as hell to step into the unknown. But you know what's scarier? Failing slowly, watching opportunities pass you by because you're too afraid to take a chance on yourself.

So here's my challenge to you—and to myself: stop waiting. Stop trying to control everything. Embrace the uncertainty. Because that's where the magic happens. That's where you find out what you're really made of. And trust me, you're made of tougher stuff than you think.

8

We spend so much of our time trying to make people like us, love us, accept us, embrace us. Showing up on social media and suddenly sharing ideas that people might not agree with or actively hate on? That shit's scary.

We've all been there, right? That moment when your finger hovers over the 'post' button, and your heart's racing like you're about to jump out of a plane. Why? Because you're about to share something that's truly you, not the polished, people-pleasing version you've carefully curated.

I've spent years—hell, decades—trying to fit in, to be the "good girl," to say the right things. It's exhausting, and you know what? It's bullshit. The day I decided to show up as my authentic self on social media was terrifying. I felt naked, exposed. What if people unfollow me? What if they leave nasty comments? What if they think I'm a fraud?

But the moment I started being real, sharing my unfiltered thoughts, calling out the BS in the online business world—that's when things shifted. Yeah, I lost some followers. But the ones who stayed? They're my people. They resonate with the real me, not some sanitized version.

It's still scary sometimes. I still get that flutter in my stomach before I hit 'post' on something controversial. But you know what's scarier? Living a half-life, always holding back, always second-guessing. Fuck that noise. Be you, unapologetically. It's the best decision you'll ever make.

9

We have learned, we have reflected, and we have done all of the things that we are supposed to do. Now is the time to actually put all of those things into action.

This has to be the year where we prioritize taking action. I'm talking about actually putting into practice all those things we've been saying we'll do "someday." No more waiting to become some idealized version of ourselves before we take the leap.

To help kickstart this action-oriented mindset, I've got ten reflection questions for you. These aren't just for navel-gazing—they're your launchpad for meaningful change:

- What are three things I'm proud of having accomplished this year?

- What have I learned that I can continue to work on next year?

- Where have I been throwing up resistance in my life or in my business? Why and what can I do to change that or embrace that?

- What am I willing to show up for or leave behind?

- Who am I going to be and what am I going to do?

- How do I want to live each day going forward?

- What is it important for me to do with my time each day or each week?

- Who deserves space in my life and who doesn't?

- Whose opinion of it all do I care about?

- What characteristics of the next version of myself do I want to cultivate next year?

Dive into these questions, but don't let them become just another paper exercise. Use them as a springboard to actually put into action all of those things you've been dreaming about. Remember, I think you know enough and I think you've done enough and I think you have enough. It's time to stop waiting and start doing.

10

You can't make a wrong decision. You can only make the decision you make because if you could have made a different decision, you would have.

I've seen so many entrepreneurs get stuck in this hellish loop of "what if" and "but maybe" that they end up doing absolutely fuck all. What if, instead of getting stuck in analysis paralysis, we accepted that there's no such thing as a wrong decision?

Every choice you make is just that—a choice. It's not some cosmic test of your worth as a business owner or a human being. It's just you, doing the best you can with the information you have at that moment. And guess what? Sometimes your best is going to look like a dumpster fire, and that's okay.

If you could have made a different decision, you would have. But you didn't. You made this one. So own it, learn from it, and move the hell on. Stop torturing yourself with coulda-woulda-shouldas.

Clarity comes from action, not overthinking. So make the damn decision. Any decision *(preferably one that's aligned for you)*. Because even if it turns out to be a shitstorm, at least you're moving forward. You can course-correct along the way.

11

You can call it conformity, code switching, making yourself palatable, playing small, whatever you want to call it. But what it comes down to is too many women were taught there is "a way" and that we aren't to deviate from that way if we want to be loved, accepted, supported, included, and so on.

Conformity is this invisible cage we've built around ourselves, and damn, it's hard to break free. I've been there, 20-plus years in a career of conformity, and let me tell you, it's exhausting.

We're told to fit in, be easy, go with the flow, be a "nice" girl, not rock the boat. And that programming runs deep. So deep that even when we strike out on our own, we find ourselves falling back into those old patterns.

What we need to remember is that we are allowed to do business the way we want to do business. And we are allowed to do life the way we want to do life. It's not about being a rebel for the sake of it. It's about honoring you, your life, and your vision.

12

Learning to trust yourself is so important. Please note that I said learning to trust yourself. A lot of us have not cultivated that ability well, or at all in some cases, because it's not something we're actually taught.

When was the last time you made a decision on your own…with no committee, no oversight, and no input from a mastermind, your biz bestie, or a coach? And if you're constantly looking to other people to help you make decisions, how the fuck are you ever supposed to develop self-trust?

We've become so damn dependent on external validation that we can't even decide what to have for lunch without polling our Instagram followers. It's like we're stuck in this perpetual cycle of seeking approval, and let me tell you, it's exhausting.

Every coach, even the ones with the best intentions, is going to coach you from their perspective, not yours, and they'll guide you according to their lived experience. That's not inherently bad, but it means you're primarily going down their path rather than forging your own.

If you're constantly in containers and not seeing progress, something is up. My guess? You don't need more coaching right now. You don't need more strategy right now. You don't need mindset work right now. You need space. You need time. You need to get clear on some shit.

It's time to take stock of where you were, what support you've gotten, where you are now, and what feels out of sync for you. Have you actually given yourself the chance to implement what you've learned? Or are you just constantly feeling the need to be supported because it's become more about seeking affirmation than actual growth?

Remember, you know the answer, but you lack the self-trust to let yourself find that answer...or you know the answer and you're afraid of what it means. Either way, it's time to face that fear. Trust yourself. Your gut knows more than you think.

13

My mission is to give women the tools they need to build sustainable BS-free businesses that allow them true freedom, true autonomy, and financial security. And audacity is the first fucking step to all of it.

I'm sick and tired of watching brilliant women get stuck in the same spot for years because they're afraid to take action.

You can invest in coaching and training and certifications all you want, but if you're not willing to step into your audacity, you're just spinning your wheels. And let me tell you, that's a fast track to nowhere.

When I created my business, I wanted total autonomy, freedom, and security, and I bet that's what you want too. But you can't get there by playing small or trying to fit into someone else's box.

That's why I'm on a mission to give women the tools they need to build sustainable BS-free businesses. I'm not here to blow smoke up your butt or sell you some magic formula. I'm here to help you tap into your audacity—that bold, brave part of you that's ready to challenge the status quo and go after what you really want.

It's not about being pushy or bitchy. It's about being clear on your worth, relentless in pursuit of your goals, and comfortable in your own skin. It's about leading with love and compassion, but also having the courage to stand up and make some noise.

14

I've never felt more confident in myself. That doesn't mean I don't get imposter syndrome. It doesn't mean that I don't have days where I feel like a fraud. It doesn't mean that I don't have days where I want to hide under a rock. But I know who I am, and I know who I want to be, and it's getting easier and easier to show up as her.

The journey of self-discovery that goes hand in hand with entrepreneurship is not for the faint of heart. Some days I wake up feeling like I could conquer the world, and other days I want to burrow under my blankets and ghost everyone. But you know what? That's okay. It's all part of the messy, beautiful process of becoming.

I used to think confidence meant never doubting yourself. What a crock of shit. Real confidence is looking your insecurities dead in the eye and saying, "Yeah, you're there. So what?" It's about embracing the journey, the constant evolution.

Every damn day, I'm peeling back another layer, uncovering another facet of who I am. It's terrifying and exhilarating all at once. And yeah, sometimes that bitch called Imposter Syndrome comes knocking. But I've learned to coexist with her. She's not the boss of me anymore.

The magic happens when you start showing up as your authentic self, warts and all. It's like giving the middle finger to all those years of trying to fit in, of dimming your light. Sure, it's scary as hell at first. But the more you do it, the easier it gets. And the payoff? It's fucking worth it.

So here I am, still figuring shit out, still growing, still occasionally feeling like a fraud. But I'm doing it openly, authentically, and unapologetically. And let me tell you, it feels good. Really good. This is me, take it or leave it. And I'm finally okay with that.

15

No woman should ever feel fear or make herself small to be palatable to the spaces she covets. No woman should feel threatened by the bigness of her sisters. Every woman can learn to love the skin she's in, regardless of age, color, size, ability, or any other arbitrary marker of division.

Growing up, I was a firework trapped in a matchbox. I spent a lot of time being told to be quiet, sit down, don't laugh so loud, stop talking, don't make so much noise. Be smaller. Don't draw attention to yourself. Every instinct to shine, to sparkle, to explode with laughter was met with a chorus of "shh" and "settle down." It was like wearing a straitjacket made of expectations—don't be too loud, too big, too much. Hell, I even rushed through networking intros like I was running to catch a train, afraid to take up too much space.

But you know what? That shit gets old. And so did I. Now, in my late forties, I'm dog-tired of shrinking. I've done the work—therapy, mentors, daily practices—to peel off those layers of "be smaller" like an onion skin of bullshit. It's not perfect. That negative self-talk bitch still shows up, but nowadays, she'll sit her ass down more often than not.

Visibility is still scary as fuck. But I've learned to speak from my scars, not my wounds. I've found my tribe of truth-tellers who get it. And I've gotten crystal fucking clear on my why: empowerment and choice.

We're here to be big, to be loud, to draw all the goddamn attention to ourselves and our sisters rising alongside us. I want to stop being afraid of her bigness, her darkness, her light, her voice. I want to stop being the dutiful daughter to all our society at large. That's my truth, and I'm done being quiet about it.

16

We spend most of our careers feeling like we have to fight for a seat at every single fucking table, fight to have our voices heard.

So many women struggle with self trust and self belief as a result of toxic workplace culture. Bad management, toxic work environments, mansplaining, being overlooked for promotion, having ideas taken without credit, hurtful criticism. I'm not being salty, just honest.

When you've gone through an entire career being trained to disregard your intuition, your instinct, your innate knowing, it can really cause you to second guess every single decision you make. Even as we start our own businesses, we still look for someone to tell us what to do, to tell us what steps to take, how to show up, where to invest, where to look. Because it takes the pressure off. It mitigates the fear of being wrong.

But remember this: You're capable, you're smart, you're talented. You are allowed to take time to rediscover yourself and your passion because entrepreneurship is one hell of a journey of self-discovery—and this time, the buck stops with you.

17

The problem with unicorns is we're all very highly prized for what we can do and not necessarily what we think, which is stupid when you think about it.

You know, I used to think being a unicorn was the shit. I could do it all—project management, graphic design, copywriting, you name it. And yeah, people loved it. They'd hire me in a heartbeat because I could wear all those hats. But they didn't give a damn about what was going on inside my head.

It took me way too long to realize that my real value wasn't in being everyone's Swiss Army knife. It was in the unique perspective I'd gained from all those experiences. The insights I'd picked up along the way. The shit I'd seen and learned that no one else had.

But the business world doesn't make it easy for us unicorns to step out of that box. They want us to stay in our lane, keep doing all the things, and shut up about our ideas. Well, fuck that noise.

It's time we unicorns started using our horns to poke holes in that bullshit narrative. Your thoughts, your ideas, your unique take on things—that's the real gold, baby. That's what's going to set you apart in a sea of cookie-cutter "experts."

So, my fellow unicorns, it's time to stop being the jack-of-all-trades and start being the master of your own damn narrative. Speak up. Share those insights. Let the world see the genius behind the skill set. Because that's where the real magic happens. That's where you stop being just another unicorn and start being a fucking legend.

18

I know too many women who are brilliant but are far too fucking humble for their own good.

For far too long, we've been fed this bullshit idea that humility is the key to success, especially for women. Well, I'm here to tell you that's a load of crap.

I've seen it time and time again—brilliant women, far too humble for their own good, watching their ideas get snatched up by louder voices. It's like we're all sitting at this giant table, but instead of speaking up, we're whispering our genius into the void, hoping someone will notice.

I hate to break it to you but no one's coming to notice you. The world doesn't work that way, especially not for women, and definitely not for women of color. We can't afford to wait for someone to stumble upon our brilliance. We need to own it, shout it from the rooftops, and stop apologizing for taking up space.

You know what happens when you play small? You get copied. Your ideas get taken. Your hard work becomes someone else's stepping stone. I've been there, and let me tell you, it sucks.

So, to hell with false humility. Embrace your genius. Stand tall in your power. It's not just about you, it's about all the voices that need to be heard. We need your perspective, your insights, your fire.

The world is waiting for you to roar.

19

Who am I waiting to become before I do the next thing that I wanna do?

I've been grappling with this question lately, and it's been blowing my mind. How many of us are constantly waiting to become someone different before taking that next step? We tell ourselves, "When I'm braver, then I will do that thing" or "When I become a better speaker, I'll launch that podcast."

What if, instead of waiting to grow into that person, we just decided to be that person right now? You wanna be a speaker? Okay, just be a speaker. You wanna sell more? Okay, sell more. Yes, there are action steps involved, but the mindset shift is crucial.

Last year, I committed to stop playing small. It's easy to say, but the work comes in asking yourself what that means tangibly. For me, it meant getting those branding photos done, even though I wasn't in the "best shape." It meant launching my podcast and putting my voice out there.

So, I'm challenging you (and myself) to stop waiting. Identify the characteristics of that future you and start cultivating them now. Or better yet, just do the damn thing and step into that version of yourself today. It's uncomfortable as hell, but trust me, it's life-changing.

Remember, I think you know enough and I think you've done enough and I think you have enough. Now it's time to take action and let this be the year that you do all the things that you have wanted to do since you started your business. Who's with me?

Part 2

IT MAY NOT BE SEXY, BUT...A BUSINESS IS A BUSINESS IS A BUSINESS

20

When you're starting out, you need three things. You need an offer. You need a way to communicate that offer, and you need a way to collect money when people buy the offer. That's it.

Look, I get it. When you're just starting out in business, it feels like you need a million things. A fancy website, a killer brand, the perfect social media strategy, and don't even get me started on all the tech tools everyone says you "must have." It's enough to make your head spin and your wallet cry.

But you don't need all that noise. Seriously. Strip it all away, and what do you actually need? An offer, a way to tell people about it, and a way to get paid. That's. Fucking. It.

Your offer? That's just what you're good at, packaged up to help someone else.

Your way to communicate? Could be as simple as talking to people or sending some emails. And collecting money? PayPal works just fine to start.

Everything else? It's just fluff. Distractions that keep you from actually doing the work and making some damn money. So many people get stuck in this loop of "getting ready to get ready" that they never actually launch. Don't be that person.

Pick a thing. Talk about it. Get paid for it. Rinse and repeat. The rest? You'll figure it out as you go.

21

A business is a business is a business. And all businesses need to be grown like a business.

I'm tired of the BS. Everyone's out here acting like online businesses are some magical unicorn that defies the laws of economics. The truth is, whether you're selling cupcakes from a storefront or coaching services from your laptop, the fundamentals are the same.

You want to grow? Great. But first, ask yourself: Do you have offers that actually work? Have you tested them? Refined them? Can you deliver consistently without burning out? These aren't sexy questions, but they are the ones that separate the businesses that thrive from the ones that nose-dive.

So before you jump on the next "scale your business to seven figures in seven days" bandwagon, take a step back. Treat your business like a real fucking business. Because at the end of the day, that's exactly what it is. No more, no less.

22

**It doesn't matter how great your marketing is
if you don't have a viable product.**

I've watched it happen time and time again in this online business space. People jump in thinking all they need is a laptop, a good idea, and a fancy personality to make money. And for a while, during that Golden Era from 2020 to 2022, they could literally fart in any direction and cash would flow. But, as hard as it can be to accept, that era is over.

Now, I'm seeing business owners scrambling. They've lost their service providers because they couldn't pay them, or worse, wouldn't listen to them. So what do they do? They double down on ineffective strategies. More posts! More offers! As if flooding social media or creating a dozen half-baked programs will magically make their business viable.

But let me tell you something—you can have the most outstanding social media team, the slickest operations, and the catchiest copywriting, but if your product is a dud, you're just putting lipstick on a pig. It doesn't matter how shiny your marketing is if you're not actually exchanging value, providing value.

This is the reckoning, people. The businesses built on ego and sand are crumbling. If you want to survive, it's time to invest in the unsexy stuff. Build a solid foundation. Create something of real value. Because at the end of the day, you succeed in business by serving your customers.

23

Getting really clear on your why is absolutely critical, and it has to be the first thing you do because it's the thing that's gonna keep you going when everything else is trying to pull you off course.

Your why doesn't have to be world-changing. Hell, it can be as simple as wanting to buy whatever the fuck you want at the bookstore without checking your bank balance. But it has to matter to you.

When you're rooted in your purpose, it's easier to say no to the bullshit. No to calls before 10 AM. No to working past school pickup. No to chasing seven figures if it means sacrificing what really matters.

So before you dive into strategies and content calendars and all that jazz, get clear on your why. It's the thing that'll keep you going when everything else is trying to pull you off course.

24

**Your mission, your vision, and your values
need to be in literally everything that you do.**

I've seen too many entrepreneurs treat their mission, vision, and values like some fancy plaque on the wall— nice to look at, but ultimately forgotten. That's bull-shit, my friends. These aren't just pretty words you cook up in a coaching program and then file away. They're the lifeblood of your business, the DNA that should infuse every decision you make.

Think about it. Your mission is your why—the reason you drag yourself out of bed every morning to face the entrepreneurial roller coaster. Your vision? That's the big, audacious dream of what becomes pos-sible when you nail that mission. And your values? They're your non-negotiables, the principles that guide you even when the path gets murky.

When I say these need to be in everything you do, I mean everything. They should shape your offers, influence who you collaborate with, and even dictate how you spend your hard-earned cash. It's not always easy, trust me. There have been times I've had to turn down seemingly golden opportunities because they didn't align with my core values. But you know what? Those decisions have kept me sane and my business authentic.

So, before you dive into planning your next big move, take a beat. Dust off that mission statement, revisit your vision, and really sit with your values. Are they still you? Do they still resonate? If not, it's okay to tweak them. You're allowed to tweak them as you continue to grow and gain clarity on what you do and why. We're all growing and changing. But once you've got that clarity? Let it be your North Star. Because a business built on a shaky foundation of misaligned values and foggy vision? That's a recipe for burnout and regret. And life's too short for that kind of BS.

25

Realistic is a dirty word in entrepreneurship. The minute you start talking about being realistic, someone's going to get pissed off. They're going to try to gaslight you into thinking your mindset is a problem, or you don't want it bad enough, or you need to try harder, or you're not willing to do the work.

I've been in this game long enough to see the eye rolls and hear the sighs when I dare to utter the word "realistic" in a room full of entrepreneurs. It's like I've cursed in church or something. But being realistic isn't the enemy of ambition—it's the backbone of sustainable success.

Every time I bring up the need for a solid business plan or suggest that maybe, just maybe, making six figures in your first month isn't a reasonable goal, I brace for the backlash. The gurus and their disciples are quick to pounce, armed with their toxic positivity and magic bullet solutions. They'll tell you your mindset is a problem, or that you don't want it bad enough, or you need to try harder, or you're not willing to do the work.

But let me tell you something—I've seen behind the curtain of those seven-figure businesses. I've untangled the mess of their backend operations and witnessed the burnout of their teams. The smoke and mirrors of overnight success stories are just that—smoke and mirrors.

Being realistic means understanding the true cost of building a business that lasts. It means respecting the expertise of your team and paying them what they're worth. It means having the patience to build a strong foundation instead of chasing the next shiny object.

So yeah, I'll keep being the voice of reason in a sea of magical thinking. Because at the end of the day, I'd rather build a business that's still standing in five years than one that collapses under the weight of unrealistic expectations.

26

You deserve the life you want, the business you want. But you deserve to do it the right way, and the right way takes time, effort, and the right support.

Look, I'm gonna give it to you straight because that's what we do here. You want success? Hell yeah, you deserve it. But let's cut the crap about overnight riches and four-hour workweeks.

I've seen too many bright-eyed entrepreneurs fall for that BS, thinking they'll be sipping mojitos by the pool while the cash rolls in. But that's not how this works. Not in your first year, probably not even in your first three to five years.

The real deal is that building a kick-ass business takes time, sweat, and yeah, sometimes tears *(usually not blood though, thankfully)*. It's not about magical thinking or manifesting abundance. It's about rolling up your sleeves and doing the work. The right work.

That means getting crystal clear on your vision, understanding your finances *(even when the numbers make you want to hide under your desk)*, and learning to be a good boss *(which, trust me, isn't always a picnic)*.

But here is the thing—you don't have to do it alone. In fact, you shouldn't. Get support. Not from some guru promising you the moon, but from people who'll give it to you straight and help you navigate the messy middle.

Because you do deserve success. You deserve a business that lights you up, that you look forward to more days than not *(let's be real, we all have our "burn it down" moments)*. Just remember, deserving it doesn't mean it falls in your lap. It means you're worthy of putting in the effort to build it right.

27

Why is it that when we work from home, we don't always take the same care in building an experience that makes it worth our while?

I had this moment of clarity the other day while listening to the news. They were interviewing this big insurance company about how they're trying to lure people back to the office. And you know what? They were making a lot of big-ticket investments in quality of experience. We're talking free fitness facility with Peloton bikes, healthy food in the cafeteria, and even on-site daycare.

And it hit me: If Big Corporate is finally making employee experience a priority, why aren't we taking the same care when we work from home?

I mean, let's be real. I've spent an inordinate amount of time eating potato chips at my desk because I haven't built in time to get away and eat a proper meal. Sound familiar?

We became entrepreneurs to reclaim autonomy and have the choice of how we fill our days. So why the hell aren't we designing an experience that makes us want to show up every day?

It doesn't have to be fancy. Maybe it's taking time in the morning to go for a walk or to the gym. Maybe it's having the ability to log off on a Friday afternoon and take some time for yourself. The what isn't as important as the how.

For me, it's been about creating little pockets of joy in my day. I'm bringing in some things to help make the space a little cozier. I'm taking breaks during the day to get outside, or at least go upstairs and grab some sun because my office is in the basement. I've got Siri reminding me to get up every hour and stretch. I've even got a basket chair and a little rocking chair in my office for each of my girls so they can come and comfortably hang out here whenever they want to.

So I want you to ask yourself: If this was a corporate job, would the current setup entice me to stay? If not, why not? What's missing?

Remember, you are your own boss. You don't need anyone's permission. You don't have to fill out a requisition, you don't have to cut any red tape. You can just decide what would bring a little more joy to your day. And then go and do the fucking thing.

28

When you constantly ditch and pivot, not only are you confusing your audience, but you're doing yourself a disservice.

I see too many business owners who legitimately have good ideas ditch and pivot too soon because they don't see immediate results. This looks like launching something and when it doesn't immediately blow up like the next TikTok dance craze, you're ready to jump to the next shiny object.

When's the last time you planted a seed and ate the fruit the same day, or even the same week, same month, even the same fucking year? That's the curse and blessing of being a visionary—you have this incredible ability to come up with fantastic ideas and create these wonderful big things, but you don't often have the patience to see that vision come to fruition.

I've seen it time and time again. It has taken some-times four, or five launches for something to actually gain the traction that is needed for it to become an "overnight success". But you're over there thinking three, four, five, even six weeks is enough to launch and promote something once and see immediate success? Honey, please. In this noisy world of endless scrolling, your putting something out there does not equal everybody seeing it and rejecting it.

So, before you jump ship on your latest brainchild, take a step back. Evaluate. Have a look. Did you promote it long enough? Did you talk about it enough? Did you tell people what you wanted them to do, aka buy your thing? Were you showing up in the right places in front of the right people?

A solid launch period is about 90 days. That seems like a long time. I know you may be thinking: You seriously want me to talk about this thing for 12 weeks? Yes, yes I do. And then I want you to do it again because most programs need to be launched multiple times to really gain traction.

Remember, there is magic in the long game, but too few entrepreneurs are actually ready or willing to wait. That can be a huge problem. Stop confusing your audience—and yourself—with constant pivots. Give your ideas room to breathe, to grow, to take root. That's how you build something that lasts.

29

Too many business owners don't know how to truly run a business that is still going to be here in three to five years.

Seeing talented entrepreneurs chase pipe dreams and quick fixes instead of building something that'll outlast the next Instagram algorithm change breaks my heart. They're so busy trying to make six figures in six days that they forget about the next six years.

And don't even get me started on how they treat their teams. I've lost count of the number of job posts I've seen offering peanuts for the moon and stars. It's like they think expertise grows on trees or something. News flash: if you want a business that's still kicking ass three to five years from now, you need to invest in people who know their shit *(and pay them what they're worth while you're at it!).*

Here's the bottom line: if you're not willing to pour your foundations, don't be surprised when your business crumbles faster than a house of cards in a hurricane. Building a sustainable business isn't sexy, but neither is going back to a 9-to-5 because your empire of sand washed away.

30

How much of what you do every day is busy work? How much of it is stuff you were told you should do or you think you have to do, but it's not resulting in any kind of ROI for your business?

We're all guilty of it—that endless hamster wheel of tasks we've convinced ourselves are crucial to our business. But here's the million-dollar question: How much of that is actually moving the needle?

I'm talking about those Instagram posts you slave over because some influencer told you consistency is key. Or that networking event you drag yourself to every month, even though you'd rather watch paint dry. Or hell, even that fancy CRM system you invested in because it's what "serious" entrepreneurs use.

But let's pause and do a little math. *(Don't worry, I promise it won't hurt.)* Take a look at your calendar from last week. Now, be brutally honest with yourself. How much of what you did each day is busy work? How many of those activities actually contributed to your bottom line? How many brought in new clients, increased your revenue, or genuinely improved your business?

If you're squirming in your seat right now, congratulations! You've just had your very own "oh shit" moment. Welcome to the club.

We've all been sold this bill of goods that being busy equals being successful. But busy doesn't pay the bills, honey. Results do.

31

We don't get to choose the ups and downs in business. We don't get to choose when the market's going to fluctuate or how much people have to invest or all of the other things that we're constantly worried about. Creating a resilient foundation keeps us grounded and it weatherproofs your business.

We all know we can't control the weather right? That's true for business too. Markets shift, trends change, and sometimes it feels like the universe is conspiring against your bank account. But you know what? That's exactly why we need to build our businesses on solid ground.

I'm talking about creating a foundation that's as sturdy as your grandma's fruitcake and as flexible as a yoga instructor. It starts with getting crystal clear on your purpose—your why. And then laser-focusing on your priorities instead of throwing spaghetti at the wall and seeing what sticks. It's about understanding your power and knowing when to ask for help. And it's about making a promise to yourself and actually keeping it.

When you've got these four P's locked down—Purpose, Priorities, Power, and Promise—you're not just building a business. You're creating a freaking fortress. One that can weather any storm, whether it's a market downturn or a global pandemic.

So stop obsessing over things you can't control. Instead, focus on building that unshakable foundation. Trust me, when the winds of change come howling *(and they will)*, you'll be the one standing tall while everyone else is scrambling for cover.

32

One of the biggest roadblocks to success in the online business space is our incessant need for instant gratification.

We're all guilty of it—that burning desire to see results NOW. It's like we've collectively forgotten that Rome wasn't built in a day, and neither is a sustainable business.

I get it. We live in a world of one-click purchases and same-day deliveries. But building a business isn't like ordering takeout, friends. It's more like cultivating a garden—it takes time, patience, and a whole lot of nurturing.

The online space is particularly treacherous. You've got gurus left and right promising six figures in six days, and it's enough to make you feel like a failure if you're not rolling in dough by Tuesday.

The truth is that success—real, lasting success—isn't about how quickly you can make a buck. It's about building something that can weather the storms, pivot when needed, and keep growing year after year. That takes time. It takes trial and error. It takes resilience.

So the next time you're tempted to throw in the towel because you haven't hit some arbitrary milestone in record time, take a breath. Remember that overnight successes are usually years in the making. Focus on building a solid foundation, not on chasing fleeting wins.

33

Successful scaling means that your growth is sustainable. So you're not just going to be making or doing more. You're also going to be making enough money to cover your increased costs and still make a profit.

Everyone's all "scale, scale, scale!" like it's some magic wand you can wave to make more money without doing more work. Wouldn't that be nice?

The thing is that scaling isn't just about pumping out more product or signing more clients. It's about growing your business in a way that doesn't make you want to tear your hair out or force you to file for bankruptcy.

Think about it. You start a cute little bakery in your kitchen. Great. But now you want to go big. You can't just quadruple your output and call it a day. You need to think about marketing, ingredients, maybe hiring help, renting a space. All of that costs money, honey.

Successful scaling means your business can handle the growth. Your systems can cope. Your team, if you have one, isn't drowning. And at the end of the day, you're not just breaking even, you're actually making a profit.

So before you jump on the scaling bandwagon, ask yourself: Is my business ready? Can I handle the increased workload? Do I have the infrastructure in place? Because if not, you're not scaling, you're just creating a bigger mess.

Remember, sustainable growth is the name of the game. Don't let anyone tell you otherwise.

34

If you really do truly honestly desire to scale your business, the most important advice I can give you: have a fucking plan.

I've seen people put more thought into their holiday planning than they do into their business growth planning. It's mind-boggling, really. You want to scale? Great. But don't come at me with some half-assed idea of just "growing" and calling it scaling. That's not how this works.

Scaling isn't just about growth. It's about being strategic, efficient, and actually increasing your profit margins while you grow. You need a plan for all seven categories of your business—yes, seven. Financial, marketing, customer experience, innovation, team growth, personal development, and operations. Miss one, and you're just setting yourself up for a cluster-fuck.

And please, for the love of all things holy, don't ignore operations. I know it's not sexy, but it's the backbone of your scaling strategy. Without solid processes and systems, you're just building a house of cards that'll come crashing down the moment you hit a snag.

Remember, only around 22% of small businesses that have been launched in the last 10 years have successfully scaled. You want to be in that group? Then get serious about your plan. Know your cash flow, understand your timeline, and for fuck's sake, stop looking for a fucking unicorn to magically fix everything.

Scaling is possible, but it's not for the faint of heart or the poorly prepared. So if you're in it to win it, buckle up, buttercup. It's time to plan like your business depends on it—because it does.

Part 3

YOU DIDN'T LEAVE YOUR NINE TO FIVE TO START A 24/7

35

You didn't leave your nine to five to start a 24/7, but that is what so many of y'all are doing.

Look, I get it. You're passionate about your business. You've got big dreams and even bigger goals. But here's the thing: when you left your 9-to-5 hustle, you didn't sign up for a 24/7 grind. Yet, that's exactly what I'm seeing so many of you do.

You're hustling, pivoting, and burning the candle at both ends. And for what? To prove you're committed? To chase some arbitrary timeline of success?

Let me tell you something—that's not what this entrepreneurial journey is about. It's about understanding your priorities and respecting your own damn capacity so you can build something that actually lights you up.

Your business should fit into your life, not the other way around. So take a breath, reassess, and remember: you're the boss now. Act like it. Set boundaries, honor your time, and for fuck's sake, stop working 24/7. Your success—and your sanity—depend on it.

36

Capacity is not just about how much time you have. It's about your financial status, how much energy you have, what your emotional and mental state are, how you physically feel on any given day and even who you have supporting you.

You know that bullshit about everyone having the same 24 hours as Beyoncé? Yeah, let's toss that out the window. When you're clear on your actual capacity—time, energy, resources, support—you stop beating yourself up for not achieving what someone else has. You're playing your own game, not theirs.

Honoring your capacity is how you create a business that doesn't leave you burnt out, resentful, and ready to throw in the towel.

How many times have you pushed through, thinking that's what successful entrepreneurs do? Spoiler alert: it's not. When you respect your limits, you create sustainable success. You're in this for the long haul, right? So act like it.

Here's another truth bomb: understanding your capacity helps you make smart decisions. When you know what you're actually working with, you can prioritize like a boss. No more wasting time on busy work or strategies that don't fit your reality. You focus on what actually moves the needle in your business.

Let's break down the pillars of capacity:

Time: Sounds simple, right? But your reality is yours alone. Stop comparing your five hours a week to someone else's fifty.

Energy: Some days you're unstoppable; others, getting up the stairs feels like climbing Everest. Honor that ebb and flow, because pushing through isn't the badge of honor we've been told it is.

Resources and Support: Do you have the right tools, knowledge, or team to get shit done efficiently? What about your support system—at home AND in your business circles?

Money: Your financial capacity isn't a measure of your worth or commitment. It's just reality, and honoring it means making smart decisions, not desperate ones.

When you start looking at capacity through these lenses, you stop playing someone else's game. You create a business that actually fits your life, not the other way around. You get to design success on your own terms, in a way that honors your values, your priorities, and yes, your limitations.

37

You deserve a business that feels aligned and full of ease. Not easy, but full of ease.

Let's get one thing straight: building a business isn't a walk in the park. It's more like hiking up a mountain with a backpack full of rocks. But what they don't tell you is that you get to choose which rocks you carry.

Too many entrepreneurs are lugging around boulders that aren't even theirs. They're following someone else's map, climbing someone else's mountain. No wonder they're exhausted and miserable.

I'm here to tell you it doesn't have to be that way. Your business should feel like it fits you, not like you're trying to squeeze into last season's skinny jeans.

When I talk about ease, I don't mean you'll be sipping margaritas on a beach while money rains from the sky. That's fantasy land, folks. I'm talking about a business that flows with your natural rhythm.

It's about doing work that lights you up, not burns you out. It's about saying "hell no" to the things that don't align, even if they look shiny on the surface. It's about building a foundation so solid that when the inevitable storms come—because they will—you're not scrambling to keep the whole damn thing from falling apart.

So take a step back. Look at your business. Does it feel like you're constantly swimming upstream? Or does it feel like you're in your element, challenges and all? You deserve a business that feels aligned and full of ease. Not easy, but full of ease. And if you're not there yet, it's time to start making some changes. Because life's too short for a business that feels like a straitjacket.

38

You get to choose when and how long you work for every single day.

In the workplace, we're taught that time equals money. The more time we spend on something, the more valuable it is. The more you hustle, the bigger the result. We're trained to account for every moment that we spent offline during the working day, every meeting that we were in, to justify our worth through our hours.

I remember having a boss who used to walk the floors every morning at 9 AM to make sure everyone was in their cubicle. And if you were a minute late, they would let you know and say, "you owe us that time at the end of the day."

But here's the thing: that mindset doesn't serve us as entrepreneurs. When you're running your own business, being chained to your desk for eight hours every day doesn't necessarily equal income or growth or even productivity.

Instead, we need to start asking ourselves: What value are you providing your clients? What activities are you engaging in for your own business that are adding value to you, your clients, or to your own business growth? It has very little to do with time spent.

As you hone your craft, you'll get more and more efficient and so charging by the hour will actually make you less money. That's why it's crucial to start thinking in terms of value, not hours.

This shift isn't easy. It took me a year to feel okay about blocking off time each morning and afternoon for school drop-off and pick-up. But by doing so, I've created space for what truly matters—both in my business and my personal life.

Remember, you get to choose when and how long you work for every single day. Your business should serve your life, not the other way around. So let go of the hustle mentality, focus on creating value, and watch how it transforms not just your business, but your entire approach to work and life.

39

You're allowed to rest. You're allowed to create ease and space in your life. You do not have to earn it.

Rest isn't a reward. It's not something you earn after you've pushed yourself to the brink. It's a necessity, like water or air. You need it to function, to think clearly, to be creative. Hell, you need it to be human.

I get it. I've been there, thinking I had to be productive every waking moment. But you know what? Slowing down has given me more clarity than any late-night work session ever did. It's shown me what really matters in my business and my life.

So here's my invitation to you: let go. Create some space. Take a damn nap if you need to. Your business won't fall apart if you're not constantly "on." In fact, it might just thrive when you give yourself the rest you deserve. Remember, you're a human being, not a human doing. Act like it.

40

Life and business are not two separate things. They're not compartmental.

I've been thinking a lot about this idea of work-life balance lately. It's bullshit, right? We're sold this narrative that we can somehow perfectly separate our work from our personal lives, but let's be real—it's all just life.

There are days when my kids need me more, when family stuff takes center stage. And you know what? That's okay. My business doesn't implode because I took a day to be present for my family. Then there are times when a big project or launch demands more of my attention, and guess what? My family survives.

The truth is, it's all interconnected. The skills I've learned in business—like setting boundaries and prioritizing—have made me a better parent. And the patience I've developed as a mom? That's been a game-changer in dealing with difficult clients.

So instead of trying to balance two separate lives, I'm learning to integrate them. Some days that means taking a client call during my kid's extracurriculars. Other days it's about closing the laptop early to have a family dinner. It's messy, it's imperfect, but it's real. And honestly? I wouldn't have it any other way. Because at the end of the day, it's all just part of building the life I want—business, family, and everything in between.

41

You deserve less.

I know, I know. It sounds crazy, right? In a world that is designed to have us pushing more, more, more, here I am, telling you that you deserve less. But stick with me for a second.

Think about your to-do list. That monster of a checklist that's always breathing down your neck. How much of that stuff actually matters? Like, really matters?

I'll let you in on a little secret: most of it doesn't. We've been sold this lie that our worth is tied to how much we can cram into a day. As if being busy is some kind of badge of honor. Only...it's not.

Here's what you really deserve:

Less stress about leaving the dishes for one night.

Less guilt about canceling on people when you're exhausted.

Less pressure to be everything to everyone, all the time.

You deserve the freedom to pick your battles. To say "not today" to the things that don't light you up. To put yourself first without feeling like you're committing some cardinal sin against productivity.

So, the next time you're about to add another "should" to your list, pause. Ask yourself: Does this matter right now? Will the world end if I don't do this? If the answer is no, give yourself permission to please your damn self.

42

Overwhelm has two main causes in business: Doing too many things, and not doing the right things.

Let's talk about overwhelm, shall we? It's that feeling of being buried or drowning under a huge mass of to-dos, that constant struggle to catch up and the day just started. I've seen it in the eyes of countless women I've consulted with, and hell, I've felt it myself.

We're all trying to dance to the hustle-focused rhythm of the online business world. We're told to post on social media every day, engage for hours, take CEO days, and oh, don't forget to double your prices while you're at it! It's exhausting, and it's bullshit.

We're either piling on tasks like we're preparing for a productivity apocalypse, or we're focusing on the wrong things entirely. Maybe we're doom scrolling instead of connecting with our ideal clients, or perhaps we're pitchslapping in DMs instead of cultivating genuine relationships.

I'm here to tell you that you don't need to do it all. You need to do what matters. Focus on your three C's: conscious cash flow, cultivating connection, and confident content. Break even consistently? That's success, baby. Show up twice a week but with content that speaks to who you are? That's golden.

43

Active patience is working as hard as you can, within your capacity, toward your goal every single day, while still acknowledging that it's going to take time.

Too many people think patience means sitting on your ass, twiddling your thumbs, and waiting for success to fall into your lap. They call it faith, mindset, or believing in yourself—but you and I both know that's not how it works.

Enter active patience. It's not about chilling and hoping your goals magically materialize. It's about giving it all you've got within your capacity, while also accepting that Rome wasn't built in a day *(or even a year)*.

Think of it like planting a Chinese bamboo tree. You water it, nurture it, care for it daily for four freaking years, and zilch happens above ground. Then bam! Year five hits, and suddenly you've got a tree shooting up three feet a day. But if you slack off during those 1400-plus days of tending? That seed's as good as dead.

That's the secret sauce of entrepreneurship right there. You keep showing up, keep nurturing your business baby, even when you can't see jack squat happening. Because you never know which day is going to be the one where your bamboo tree finally breaks through the soil and starts its crazy growth spurt.

So yeah, be patient. But make it active patience. Work your tail off, stay consistent, and trust the process. Because that's how you build a business that doesn't just sprout—it freaking thrives.

44

Done is better than perfect, yes, but peace of mind is even better.

Don't get me wrong, I'm not saying we should half-ass everything. But there's a sweet spot between "done" and "perfect" that we often overlook. It's called "good enough with peace of mind."

Think about it. What could you let go of in your business that's stealing your peace? Maybe it's how you show up on social, how you price your offers, how you share your content or work with clients, how you structure your day, where you take breaks, or even just how you run your business in general. What if, instead of chasing perfection, we chased contentment? What if we valued our peace of mind as much as our output?

So that's my challenge to you *(and to myself)*: Find that thing you're obsessing over, that thing that's robbing you of your joy, and let it go. Choose peace over perfection.

45

Work life balance is, in fact, bullshit. It's a giant myth. There is no such thing as work life balance.

Work-life balance implies having an equal amount of time for both work and home. And I don't care who you are, it is never that fucking simple. We've been sold this elusive dream for decades, and I'm calling bullshit on it. Life is messy, unpredictable, and beautifully chaotic. It doesn't fit into neat little boxes or perfectly balanced scales.

The whole concept carries this weird expectation of constant exchange. If I'm working hard, then I need to do things to allow me to play just as hard. Or if I'm spending an afternoon off work hanging out with the kids, then I have to do something to make up that time at work later on that week. It's like we're all amateur accountants, frantically trying to balance the books of our lives. But here's the thing: our capacity fluctuates daily, sometimes hourly. Some days, I'm a productivity powerhouse; others, I'm lucky if I remember to eat lunch.

Instead of chasing this mythical balance, I propose we embrace the ebb and flow of our energy and priorities. You get to decide what works, and you get to decide what each working day looks like. Maybe today you need a three-hour lunch break to recharge. Tomorrow, you might be in the zone and work until midnight. That's okay. You don't need anyone's permission. You're the CEO of your life, so start acting like it. Ditch the guilt, forget the balancing act, and start designing days that honor your values, capacity, and the beautiful mess that is real life.

46

Sometimes rest—as in, not doing the thing—is the quickest way to doing the thing.

It's taken me years to actually believe this, but sometimes, not pushing yourself is the quickest way to find answers. It's counterintuitive, right? We're programmed to think that constant hustle is the key to success. But I've learned that when I give my brain a break, when I lean into rest, the right answers come much more easily and quickly.

This doesn't mean I'm not working or thinking about my business. It's more like I'm allowing my brain to do its thing in the background while I focus on other stuff—like cooking for my family or just being present. It's uncomfortable at times, especially for someone like me who's traditionally been all about productivity. But I'm learning that this discomfort is where the magic happens.

47

If you lose momentum from posting on social media or engaging with people in your Facebook group or whatever, yeah, the algorithm might temporarily deprioritize your stuff, but once you get going again after an initial burst of effort, it'll pick you back up and you'll be right back where you started.

Momentum in business is a lot like riding a bicycle. When you start riding a bicycle, it's a little tougher at the beginning, right? To pedal and get the momentum going, those pedals are a little bit harder. You've got to put more exertion in. But once you're cruising, it's smooth sailing.

When you stop pedaling, your bike doesn't fall apart. The wheels don't go flying off, the handlebars don't crumble. It just eventually...stops. And that's okay. Because when you get your feet back on the pedals, it takes a little extra effort to get going again. But once you're going, that momentum starts to pick up and you're cruising again.

This is what happens when you take a break from your business. And the reason for that break? It is yours alone. You don't have to justify it to anyone.

So, give yourself grace and stay the course. Because when you come back, when you're ready to pedal again, you'll be right back where you started. And isn't that the whole point of this entrepreneurial game? To build a business that works for you, not the other way around? You get to decide how hard you want to pedal, and when you want to coast. And anyone who tries to shame you for that? Well, they can take a long ride off a short pier.

48

You have the right and the freedom to set rules about how clients will engage with you.

When I first started my business, I thought I had to be available for clients 24/7 to be successful. I was constantly answering emails, jumping on last-minute calls, eating lunch at my desk, and bending over backward to accommodate every client request.

I was recreating the corporate world I'd just left, and it was suffocating me. Sound familiar?

Then I discovered a game-changer: the "what it's like to work with me" document a.k.a. your business boundaries manifesto.

This document specifies your working hours, the holidays you'll be taking, how you prefer to communicate, and the times that you'll be doing that. It's basically your professional boundaries on paper.

It took me three years to write mine, to actually include the fact that I have kids, they'll be in the zoom room once in a while, and if that's a problem, we can't work together. That's right, it's in my document—no apologies, no hiding.

By clearly communicating your boundaries and expectations, you're setting the foundation for healthier, more productive client relationships.

Beyond that, it is about owning your worth and your time. Remember, you work with your clients, not for them. You are as much a business owner as they are, even if your business is providing them a service.

So, if you haven't already, take some time to craft your "what it's like to work with me" document. Be clear, be firm, and most importantly, be you. Trust me, your future self (and your clients) will thank you for it.

49

A lot of us grew up feeling like asking for help was a weakness… and it's not. It's actually a superpower, because you're honoring the limits of your capacity.

As super ambitious, type A women, we take everything onto ourselves. We've got more plates spinning than a circus act, and God forbid we ask for help.

But then we also get pissed off when nobody helps us. Well, why would people help you when you're a fucking superwoman and you can do all the things yourself?

We've been sold this lie that asking for help is weak. That needing support somehow makes us less badass. But you want to know what's really weak? Burning yourself out because you're too damn stubborn to admit you're human.

Newsflash: You are not infinitely powerful. You are a human being with very human limits. And guess what? Recognizing those limits isn't a weakness—it's actually a superpower.

When you ask for help—whether it's from mentors or coaches or biz besties or team members or investors, or an accountability buddy—you're not admitting defeat. You're strategically expanding your capacity. You're saying, "Hey, I'm smart enough to know I don't know everything."

So here's your permission slip: Stop being a martyr. And definitely stop getting pissed when no one offers to help your superwoman self. Instead, get comfortable with being uncomfortable. Ask for that support. Seek out that accountability. Make those investments in yourself.

Because that, my friend, is how you truly honor your power. That's how you build a business—and a life—that doesn't leave you burnt out and resentful.

Part 4

UNICORNS, PITCHSLAPS, GET-RICH-QUICK SCHEMES AND OTHER BS FROM THE BUSINESS TRENCHES

50

This isn't fucking Costco. You don't get free samples. If you want to see people's work, you pay for their work. It's that simple.

I've heard so many stories from service providers who've been asked to do "test projects" or provide "work samples" during interviews. And let me tell you, it pisses me off. Why? Because it's bullshit, that's why.

Here's the thing: when you're hiring someone, especially for a freelance gig, you're not just buying a product off the shelf. You're investing in someone's skills, their time, their expertise. And that shit has value. Real, tangible value.

I've seen web designers pour their hearts into creating entire websites, only to have clients try to weasel out of paying by claiming the site was "hacked" or some other nonsense. I've heard of operations people doing months of work, setting up entire systems, training team members, only to wake up to a charge-back notice for tens of thousands of dollars. It makes me physically ill to think about it.

And you know what? This isn't just about the money. It's about respect. It's about recognizing that there are actual human beings on the other end of these services, these businesses. People with bills to pay, families to feed, dreams to pursue.

When you ask for free work, you're saying, "Hey, your time isn't valuable. Your skills aren't worth any-thing unless I say they are." And that's some grade-A bullshit right there.

Now, I get it. You want to make sure you're hiring the right person. But guess what? That's what portfo-lios are for. That's what references are for. Hell, that's what paid trial periods are for if you really need to see someone in action.

And let's be real for a second. If you're a business owner who can't stomach paying for a small trial project, how the hell are you going to handle paying for ongoing work? It's a red flag, my friends. A big, waving, "I'm gonna be a nightmare client" red flag.

So here's my advice: If you're a service provider, stand your ground. Your work has value. Period. Don't let anyone tell you otherwise. And if a potential client balks at paying for your time and expertise, well, maybe they're not the kind of client you want to work with anyway.

And if you're a business owner looking to hire? Be prepared to pay for what you're asking for. It's not just the right thing to do, it's good business. Because when you respect people's work and pay them fairly, you build relationships. You build trust. And in this crazy world of online business, that's worth its weight in gold.

51

You cannot give yourself the title of thought leader. That is something that is bestowed upon you by the people when they actually see you as having leading thoughts.

Alright, let's cut through the bullshit and talk about thought leadership. This term has been thrown around so much in the online space, it's practically lost all meaning. It's like everyone woke up one day, decided they had a semi-original idea, and bam! Suddenly they're a "thought leader." Spoiler alert: that's not how it works.

Here's the deal: having a strong opinion doesn't make you a thought leader. It makes you opinionated. Congratu-fucking-lations, join the club. We've all got opinions.

Let me break it down for you with a classic example: the whole "paid ads versus organic growth" debate in online business. I've seen people plant their flag firmly in one camp or the other and declare themselves thought leaders. "Organic growth is the only way!" they proclaim. Or, "Paid ads or bust!" they shout from the rooftops.

But that's not leading thought. That's just picking a side. It's like choosing between pizza and tacos and thinking you've solved world hunger.

Real thought leadership? It's messier. It's more nuanced. It doesn't require you to agree with my side of the story. In fact, it doesn't even really take a side of the story. Leading thought means looking at the whole damn picture and saying, "Hold up. Here's what we're all missing."

It's about pushing yourself out of your comfort zone, but not by being a contrarian asshole or stirring up shit for the sake of engagement. It's about being okay with people maybe not liking you a little bit because you're calling out the emperor's new clothes.

True thought leadership is about synthesizing perspectives, insights, and experiences to pull out that unique angle that everyone else is overlooking. It's about moving the conversation forward when everyone else is stuck in a loop.

So, you want to be a thought leader? Here's your wake-up call: Stop trying to fit into the mold of what you think a thought leader should be. Stop waiting for someone to hand you a badge that says "Certified Thought Leader."

Instead, start showing up as authentically as you can. Tap into your why, your purpose, your values. Speak the truth that's burning inside you, the one that makes you a little afraid to say out loud. Have the guts to ask the questions no one else is asking, to point out the elephant in the room, to connect the dots that everyone else is missing.

Be the voice that makes people stop and think, "Damn, I've never looked at it that way before." That's how you become a real thought leader, not just another self-proclaimed guru in a sea of sameness.

52

I get that there is an element of convincing in sales, but it shouldn't be at the expense of someone's dignity and their financial security.

What is it with making me commit to a long ass application form or to jumping through a bunch of hoops or getting on a call before you give me a fucking price?

Look, I get it. Getting me on a call first allows you to sell to me. It allows you to handle my objections or my hesitations. It's all about those high pressure tactics, right? But here's the thing: most people know what they can afford. And they shouldn't have to turn into Sherlock fucking Holmes to figure out if they can work with you.

I remember when I was starting out, I got on a call with someone only to find out it was a five figure investment. I wasn't about to take out a loan or rob from

Peter to pay Paul. But you know what happens? Unless you're really strong and well-boundaried, you end up feeling guilty for wasting their time and maybe even say "yes" to something you can't afford.

If you're trying to make a decision about an investment and you feel a sense of urgency or desperation around it, it's probably your intuition telling you it's not the right investment at this time.

And when you're on the other side of the table: put your fucking price on your sales page. Let people know what it's going to cost them. If your offer is good, people who can afford it will see the value.

And those who can't? They might save up to work with you later when they can focus on what you're trying to teach them instead of worrying about the money.

At the end of the day, it's about respect. Respect for your potential clients' time, their financial situation, and their ability to make informed decisions. You do not want people to take out a loan to work with you. If you're truly offering value, you don't need to hide behind secretive pricing. Let your work speak for itself, and let people decide if it's right for them. That's how you build a business with integrity.

53

I'm tired of being made to feel like I have to look and speak and post a certain way. Do you remember when there was all that backlash against the curated pics on Instagram and everyone said get authentic and get vulnerable? But then the authenticity and the vulnerability was also curated?

It's like we're all stuck in this bizarre online business funhouse mirror. Every time we think we're breaking free from one mold, we're just cramming ourselves into another. Remember when we all collectively rolled our eyes at those picture-perfect Instagram feeds? We demanded authenticity, vulnerability, the "real" stuff. And what did we get? Perfectly curated authenticity. It's fucking exhausting.

Here's the thing: we're also fucking afraid to be the real us. We're told to be authentic, but only the right kind of authentic. Vulnerable, but not too vulnerable. Real, but make it marketable. It's all just another performance, another mask we're expected to wear.

This isn't just about how we look or what we post. It seeps into everything—how we operate within the confines of our own businesses. We're all trying to fit into these predefined boxes of what a "real" entrepreneur should be, should do, should want.

But here's what I'm realizing: true authenticity isn't about fitting into anyone else's mold, even if that mold is labeled "authentic." It's about stripping away all of that. Going back to basics, and figuring out who you are, what you want, and why. Not what some guru tells you to want, not what looks good on Instagram, but what resonates with your core truth, your singularity.

So yeah, I'm ready to do business how I want to fucking do it. And if that doesn't fit into someone else's idea of what an entrepreneur should be? Well, that's their problem, not mine.

54

No, you don't always need to have a coach.

Look, I get it. The coaching industry has drilled into our heads that we always need someone guiding us, holding our hands through every business decision. But here's the thing—sometimes you need to trust your own damn voice.

I've been there, constantly jumping from one coach to another, thinking each new perspective would be the magic bullet. But you know what? There came a point where I realized I was using coaching as a crutch. I couldn't make a decision without running it by someone else first. Where's the self-trust in that?

Don't get me wrong, coaches can be fantastic. But there's a fine line between support and codependency. Sometimes, you need to step back, take a breather, and listen to your own instincts. It's in those quiet moments, free from the noise of constant advice, that you might just find the answers you've been searching for.

So, if you're feeling stuck or resistant to your current coaching situation, consider this your permission slip to take a break. Give yourself space to integrate what you've already learned and been coached around and then take action and see how it feels. You might be surprised at how much wisdom you've already got tucked away in that beautiful brain of yours.

Remember, it's your business, your vision. Don't let someone else's path become your detour. Trust yourself. You got this.

55

A pitchslap is not a form of connection.

Let me paint you a picture of the online business world's equivalent of a bad Tinder date. You're minding your own business, scrolling through your DMs, when BAM! Some rando slides in with a generic "Hey, gorgeous! You're killing it in business!" followed by a pitch for their "life-changing" program.

Newsflash, folks: This is not connection. It's the digital version of walking into a room and throwing business brochures at people's faces. It's about as appealing as a root canal performed by a toddler with a spork.

Here's the tea: Sales are the byproduct of genuine connection. But too many people are treating relationships like a one-night stand when they should be aiming for a long-term romance. They want to see an

ROI right away, forgetting that in the relationship game, nothing immediate ever bears fruit worth picking.

So, how about we ditch the pitchslapping and start cultivating authentic connections? Take the time to create safety and trust. Engage with people, but don't treat those engagements like you're trying to hit it and quit it. Unless, of course, that's your thing—in which case, I have no idea why you're here.

56

If I don't have something to say that I feel like you're gonna get value from, I'm not gonna send the thing, I'm not gonna post the thing or share the thing.

You know, I've been wrestling with this idea of content creation lately. It's like this constant pressure in the online business world—post daily, send weekly emails, always be visible. But I'm not about that life.

I've had a Facebook community for years, because that's what you you're supposed to do, right? But maintaining it has been such a hard slog. I found myself struggling to be in there consistently, to provide the kind of value that I felt obligated to give. And it got me thinking—why am I doing this?

I don't want to be posting content just for the sake of posting content. It's the same with emails. If I don't have something to say that I feel like you're gonna get value from, I'm not gonna send the thing, I'm not gonna post the thing or share the thing.

This approach might seem counterintuitive in a world that's all about constant engagement. But I think it's time we challenge that norm. It's about quality over quantity, about respect for your time and attention.

So, I'm embracing this new way of thinking. I'm letting go of the pressure to constantly produce and instead focusing on creating things that truly matter. Because at the end of the day, isn't that what we're all after? Real connection, real value, real growth.

It might mean I'm not as visible, but when I do show up, you can bet it'll be worth your time. That's my promise to you, and to myself.

57

Yeah, bitch, that's right. I'm not fully invested in you, your product or your business. I'm partially invested at this number of hours for this dollar amount. Why is that a problem?

This whole "all in" bullshit has gotten way out of hand. CEOs and founders are out here acting like they own your soul just because they cut you a check for services rendered. They don't.

Here's the deal: as a service provider, when I sign up for a job, I'm making a trade. My time and skills for your money. It's a transaction, not a blood oath. And yet, these business owners lose their minds the moment you dare to have a life outside their precious little empire.

What's the problem with me having my own pod-cast? Or doing speaking engagements? Or, hell, even having hobbies that don't revolve around your company? It doesn't mean I'm not committed. It means I'm a whole-ass person with interests and ambitions beyond your bottom line.

The audacity of these people thinking they can dictate what I do in my own time is mind-boggling. Sorry, not sorry, but my life doesn't revolve around your business 24/7. I'll give you my best during working hours, but after that? My time is my own.

It's high time we stopped equating partial investment with lack of commitment. You want my full attention during work hours? You got it. But don't expect me to eat, breathe and sleep the business. That's not dedication—that's delusion.

So yeah, I'm partially invested. I'm invested exactly as much as you're paying me to be. And if that's a problem for you? Well, maybe it's time to check your expectations, not my commitment.

58

Too many people rely on their aura, their celebrity, to justify their price points and not the actual content or real value of the offer.

Let me tell you something that might ruffle some feathers in the online business world: Just because someone's a big name doesn't mean their offer is worth a damn.

I've seen behind the curtain. Some of these "celebrity entrepreneurs" are selling you a load of crap wrapped in a shiny package. They're trading on their name, but what they're actually delivering from a content perspective is a shit sandwich. It's nothing that would warrant that kind of price tag.

Here's the truth: Your fancy name means squat if you're not delivering real value. I don't care if you've got a million followers or if Oprah once sneezed in your direction. What matters is the transformation you're providing, the results you're getting for your clients.

If you're thinking about investing in a high-ticket offer, don't get dazzled by the sparkle. Dig deeper. Ask the uncomfortable questions. What exactly are you getting for your money? How hands-on is the experience? And for the love of all that's holy, don't fall for the "you're investing in me" bullshit. You're not marrying them, you're buying a service.

Remember, high price does not automatically equal high value. Sometimes, it just means you're paying for someone's ego trip. And honey, that's not a ride you want to be on.

59

I fucking hate unicorns.

You know who I'm talking about, that mythical team member who can do it all—organize files, do data management, rock graphic design, run social media, nail the copywriting, manage a launch and also do some client facing work. Sounds great, right? Wrong.

I've been that unicorn because I can do a lot of things, wearing all those hats, playing all those roles. And let me tell you, it's a trap. Sure, it might seem like a dream for business owners, especially when you're just starting out. One person to cover all the bases? Sign me up! But it's a slippery slope to exploitation.

Think about it. We've always been told that the more that you can do the more valuable you are. But that mindset is toxic as hell. It opens the door to being overworked, underpaid, and underappreciated. We end up stretched thin, trying to be everything to everyone, and losing sight of our true strengths and passions.

It's time to call bullshit on the unicorn myth. We're not magical creatures here to solve all your business problems. We're professionals with unique skills, perspectives, and limits. So instead of hunting for unicorns, how about we start valuing people for their specific talents and treating them like the badass humans they are?

60

You are not going to make $20,000 a month on four hours a week while you sip mojitos by the pool in your first year, maybe not even in your first three to five years.

Alright, let's have a come-to-Jesus moment.You know those Instagram posts showing some guru working from a beach in Bali, claiming they made six figures last month from their laptop? And because they did it, you can too...yeah, that's a crock of shit.

Look, I'm not here to rain on your parade. I want you to succeed. But I want you to succeed in the real world, not some fantasy land cooked up by marketers trying to sell you the next get-rich-quick scheme.

Building a business is hard work. It's late nights, early mornings, and a whole lot of "what the hell am I doing?" moments in between. It's learning to be a good boss *(spoiler alert: you might be a bit of an asshole at first),* figuring out finances when numbers make your head spin, and realizing that "passive income" isn't so passive after all.

But you know what? That's okay. Because while you might not be sipping mojitos by the pool in year one, you're building something real. Something that's yours.

So ditch the fantasy. Embrace the grind. And remember, those "overnight successes" you see? They're never overnight successes. I promise you, there is no such thing. Now, let's roll up our sleeves and build a business that actually lasts longer than a suntan.

61

Hire people and pay them properly or don't hire them at all.

I've been having a lot of conversations lately about this bullshit trend of underpaying people in the name of "business growth." I have seen big name coaches who are making multimillions of dollars, right? And they're over there bragging about the fact that they're paying their team members $10 or even $15 an hour, and it makes me want to scream.

If you can't afford to pay someone more than that, then you can't afford to hire them. Period. End of story. If you are hiring support in your business, it should be with the desire to pay them a living wage. At the very least.

And don't even get me started on those who think it's okay to pay peanuts to overseas workers. Shove your savior complex back up your ass. Yeah, I said it. Do not deny people the dignity of valuing their work just because they don't live in your country. There is no justification for paying them so little just because their cost of living is different or seemingly less than it is here.

You'll hear these same people talk about their values and how they honor and respect women, and they want to lift all women up, and then they don't even pay their teams a living wage. The hypocrisy is staggering.

Look, if you're not ready to pay people properly, maybe you hire in an ops expert on a short term basis to help you streamline your back end so that you can work more efficiently without a team member. Or maybe you need to rethink your business model altogether.

But whatever you do, don't build your empire on the backs of underpaid workers. It's not just unethical, it's unsustainable. Pay people properly or do it your damn self. That's the bottom line. No exceptions, no excuses.

62

Please stop buying into the fallacy of massive value. You know what I'm talking about, right? If I just give them a ton of stuff, they will see how amazing I am and they will buy. No, they won't.

You've heard it a million times: give away your best stuff for free and people will be so impressed, they'll jump for your paid thing.

But the truth is, all those "clients" you keep courting with your free and low ticket shit are not going to buy your high ticket offer no matter how much they love you or how much value you've showered them with.

Why? Because your high ticket audience does not does not have the same problems, needs, or budgets. Hell, they don't even have the same desired outcomes.

Let me break it to you gently—your lowest price consumer is also often your least loyal consumer. There's no magical loyalty equals sales formula here. That $20 buyer isn't going to morph into a $5,000 client just because you gave them a ton of freebies.

So, what's the solution? Get intentional, for fuck's sake. Stop trying to be everything to everyone. Your higher ticket stuff needs a very specific message and audience and your lower ticket and free stuff needs a very specific audience and message, and nary the twain shall meet.

When you compare how much work you're putting into something, how much time you are giving of yourself, how much time you are spending building resources, if you are not making at least that in return, you're not a profitable business. You're just running yourself into the ground.

It's time to stop the value vomit and start being strategic. Your bank account will thank you.

63

You can't be a thought leader if you don't have a clue.

Look, I'm going to say a thing, and it might ruffle some feathers, but someone's got to say it. We've got a whole bunch of so-called "thought leaders" in this online space who couldn't lead a thought if it came with a leash and treats.

Back in the day, the online business space was flooded with "experts" selling the dream without actually living it. It was like a pyramid scheme of bullshit— coaches teaching coaches to coach, and people making bank by telling you how to make bank, all without actually teaching anything. It was the blind leading the blind, but with better lighting and a fancy Instagram filter. Now, these same folks are trying to rebrand themselves as "thought leaders" and "experts."

But here's the kicker—they've never done any-thing but build their own business, if that, and let's be real, it probably wasn't even successful. They don't un-derstand the nuance, the grit, the unsexy stuff that goes into building something that lasts.

Thought leadership cannot exist if you do not have expertise and authority in a particular niche. It's born from experience, from falling on your face and getting back up, from actually doing the damn thing.

So, to all you aspiring thought leaders out there, I've got one piece of advice: before you start leading, make sure you know where the hell you're going.

64

Passive income is often touted as a get rich quick tactic, which is absolute BS. In fact, all get rich quick tactics are BS.

Let's get real about passive income. We're all chasing this dream of making money effortlessly, right? The problem is, that's a load of crap.

I've seen countless "gurus" flashing their overnight success stories, but the stats prove them wrong. Only about 20% of American households earn passive income, and most of that is through things like dividends or rental properties. We're talking a median of around $4,200 per year. Not exactly early retirement money, is it?

Now, let's talk digital products. The average Udemy income is around $3,300 per year. Their own stats show that only 1% of their thousands of instructors make a full-time income selling courses. And even that "full-time income" is around $50,000 a year. Not exactly the millionaire lifestyle we're sold, huh?

Creating something quality takes a ton of time, sometimes months or years. It's not just the hundreds of hours it can take to create and continually improve, but the market research ahead of time as well. And guess what? Just because you build it doesn't mean they're going to come.

There was an article a while back in the New York Times about a guy who tried to set up an online golf store. He spent about $5,000 on sourcing and testing products, created a website, and put in hours setting everything up. After the first year, he'd only made $300 in sales. That's a $4,700 loss, not counting all the time he invested.

So let's stop calling it passive income, because it's not passive. Let's call it what it is: a secondary income stream. And if you're thinking about diving in, ask yourself some hard questions first:

- How big is my audience?

- Do I have credibility in the space?

- Have I already sold a product or service successfully multiple times?

- What is my audience asking for that I can package into something evergreen?

- How am I going to support buyers after they purchase?

- What's the total resource cost to create and maintain this?

- Do I have the skills or team needed to create and continually market it?

- And most importantly: Is chasing this really the best use of my time, money, and energy right now?

The bottom line? Diversify your income streams. That's the real key to achieving what you're after. Stop chasing unicorns and start focusing on building real, sustainable income streams. Because at the end of the day, there's no such thing as easy money—just smart work and strategic planning.

65

A one to many program is the quickest way to scale an offer and make money. It absolutely is. The problem is that too many people offering one to many are simply not ready to do it.

I get it, the allure of scaling quickly is tempting but we need to stop offering group programs so fucking soon. Rushing into offering a group program without proper preparation is like trying to run before you can crawl. It's a recipe for disaster.

Buying into the "quick and dirty" offering myth is the reason why there are so many crap courses and programs that people leave or don't finish or stop showing up for. And let me tell you, that's not scaling your business—it just becomes the quickest way to screw your reputation and tank your business.

Look, I'm not saying group programs are bad. They can be fantastic when done right. But you've got to put in the work first. Get your hands dirty with one-on-one work. Set solid foundations. Figure out how you want to feel, your values, your priorities, your capacity, all of that stuff. That's why we do the work.

So before you jump on the group program bandwagon, ask yourself: Have I really done the groundwork? Because if you haven't, you're not just shortchanging your clients—you're shortchanging yourself and your business.

What does the groundwork look like? Glad you asked:

- You've tested your process with multiple one-on-one clients
- You've achieved repeatable results
- You've developed a process that actually delivers
- You've worked through that process multiple times
- You've ironed out the wrinkles
- You've tweaked and perfected your program

66

A good offer stands on its own legs. You don't need to throw 37 freebies at it to inflate its value and make it look like I'm getting one hell of a deal from a money perspective.

Let's talk about this ridiculous trend of padding out offers with a metric ton of "bonuses." You know what I'm talking about, right? You're selling a thing. Could be a workshop, a webinar, a class, you know, something similar. And the thing itself is maybe $500. But wait, there's more!

In order to get people to buy, to entice them to buy, what do you do? You add a bunch of bonuses. A whole bunch of freebies, maybe videos, downloadables. They get access to a calendar or a calculator or a chatbot. And suddenly, your $500 offer comes with $14,000 worth of freebies as bonuses. Fuck off.

Let's be real here, how many people actually use all of those freebies? I have yet to meet one. It's rare to get freebies or bonuses that actually add value to a person's business. Usually it's shit someone created for some other reason that they're throwing together to pad out their offer.

If you're unwilling or unable to create an offer that stands on its own, you're not ready to sell it. Instead of throwing 37 freebies at your offer, work on your offer, make your offer so good that people buy the offer without having to be enticed into it with a shit ton of bonuses.

What would actually be valuable? A one to one call. Something that helps people implement what they're buying. But if you don't have the capacity for that, don't worry about adding freebies at all. Focus on making your core offer irresistible.

So the next time you're tempted to pad out your offer with a bunch of bullshit bonuses, stop and ask yourself: Is my offer good enough on its own? If it's not, fix that first. That's how you create real value, not this inflated nonsense that nobody actually uses.

67

Your worth has nothing to do with it. You, my friend, are infinitely worthy and we really need to get away from this idea of charging based on our inherent value.

I'm so fucking tired of hearing coaches tell people to "charge their worth." It's bullshit, plain and simple. Your worth as a human being is infinite, immeasurable, and has absolutely nothing to do with how much you charge for your services.

When you tie your pricing to your self-worth, you're setting yourself up for a world of hurt. One day you're feeling like a million bucks, so you jack up your prices. The next day, imposter syndrome hits, and suddenly you're questioning everything. It's a roller-coaster that'll make you dizzy and leave your business in shambles.

Instead, let's talk about what really matters: the value you bring to your clients. Your experience, your results, the transformation you offer—that's what you should be using as a basis for your pricing. It's not about you; it's about what you can do for them.

So, the next time some guru tells you to "charge your worth," I want you to look them dead in the eye and say, "My worth is priceless, but my services? They're priced based on the value I deliver." And then walk away like the badass you are, because you just committed some serious business blasphemy.

Part 5

THIS ENTREPRENEUR SH!T IS NOT FOR THE FAINT OF HEART

68

There are days when I hate my business.

We've all heard those gurus preaching about 'following your passion' and how your business should light you up every damn day. But that's bullshit.

Running a business isn't all unicorns and rainbows. There are days when I want to burn it all down, slam the door, and sit in the dark by myself. And you know what? That's normal. It's fucking normal.

Your business is not gonna light you up every single fucking day of the week. You are not gonna eject yourself out of bed every morning because your passion burns so brightly.

And guess what? That is totally okay. It's okay to have days when you hate your business. It's okay to not feel lit up every single day. What matters is that when you zoom out, when you do an honest audit of your journey, you can see that core essence of why you're in business in the first place.

So yeah, some days suck. But other days? Other days leave me with such a sense of gratitude and fulfillment that it makes all the bullshit worth it.

69

Never be so married to something—whether it's a plan, a course of action, or whatever—that, if things don't go the way you want or expect, you aren't able to adapt.

As entrepreneurs, we're constantly bombarded with messages about the importance of having a solid strategy, a foolproof plan, a fucking roadmap to success. And don't get me wrong, planning has its place. But life doesn't give a shit about your plans.

You know what happens to most of those meticulously crafted five-year business plans? They become really expensive coasters. Because the market shifts, technology evolves, or a global pandemic decides to crash the party. Surprise, bitches!

The real superpower in business isn't planning—it's adaptability. It's being able to pivot faster than a ballerina on Red Bull when things go sideways. And trust me, things will go sideways. They always do.

This doesn't mean you shouldn't plan at all. Hell no. But hold those plans loosely, stay flexible, stay open, and for fuck's sake, don't get so attached to your plans that you miss the forest for the trees.

70

We can sit here and say when you know better, you do better. But we don't always know how to do better.

Look, I've been in this online business space long enough to see some shit. And let me tell you, it's not always pretty. We've got clients initiating chargebacks like it's a fucking sport, people expecting miracles on impossible timelines, and don't even get me started on the ones who think "free sample" applies to skilled labor.

But here's the thing: I don't believe most people wake up thinking, "How can I be an absolute dick to my service provider today?" Nah, it's not that simple. Sometimes, they just don't know any better. They're running their first business, learning as they go, and yeah, sometimes they fuck up.

That's why I'm all about having those crucial con-versations. Not the passive-aggressive email chains or the awkward ghosting dance. I'm talking real, honest-to-god, grown-up conversations. Because how else are we supposed to learn and grow?

It's easy to sit here and preach "when you know better, you do better," but that's bullshit if we're not willing to have the tough talks. So let's cut the crap, put on our big kid pants, and start communicating. Maybe then we can actually build businesses that don't make us want to tear our hair out every other day. Just a thought.

71

The work is up to you. The effort that you put in is up to you. Staying focused is up to you. What is not up to you is the timeline.

I've spent 14 years trying to make a move happen. 14 years of false starts, obstacles, and disappointments. It's enough to make anyone throw in the towel. But here's the thing: I didn't.

Why? Because I knew, deep in the heart of my hearts, that this was meant to be. It wasn't about forcing it or rushing it. It was about persistence, about showing up every day and doing the work, even when it felt like we were getting nowhere.

Life's funny like that. You think you're in control, that if you just push hard enough, you can make things happen on your timeline. But that's not how it works.

The universe, God, whatever you want to call it, has its own schedule.

What we can control is our effort, our focus, our willingness to keep trying. Everything else? That's out of our hands. It's a hard lesson to learn, especially in this world of instant gratification. But when you finally get it, when you let go of the need to control every little thing, that's when the magic happens.

So here's my advice: do the work, stay focused, and trust the process. The timeline isn't up to you, but your persistence is. And sometimes, when you least expect it, everything happens so quickly that you're left wondering why you ever doubted in the first place.

72

Assertiveness is actually a crucial aspect of leadership, because it allows you to lead not only with confidence, but with integrity.

I used to think being a badass boss meant taking no prisoners and scaring the crap out of everyone. Yeah...I was wrong.

Assertive leadership doesn't mean being the loudest in the room. It means confidently standing your ground while respecting others' ideas. It's saying, "This project needs more time for quality," without apology or aggression.

When you lead assertively, you create space for your team to engage, not just comply. People don't just follow you; they trust you. They grow with you.

73

Your mindset is fine. What fucks with your mindset is the BS in the space about how easy it is for everyone else.

I'm so fucking tired of hearing gurus tell you that your business isn't thriving because your mind ain't right. It's bullshit, plain and simple. Your mindset isn't the problem—it's the toxic sludge of misinformation you're swimming in that's messing with your head.

Every day, you're bombarded with stories of overnight successes, six-figure launches, and entrepreneurs living their best lives by the pool. It's enough to make anyone feel like a failure. Until you realize that most of it is smoke and mirrors.

The truth? Building a business is hard work. It's messy, it's frustrating, and sometimes it feels like you're moving backwards. That's normal. What's not normal is expecting to hit seven figures in your first year just because some coach with a fancy Instagram feed told you she did it.

So, stop beating yourself up. Your mindset is probably just fine. It's the unrealistic expectations and the constant comparison that's screwing with you. Focus on your own journey, celebrate your own wins, no matter how small, and for the love of all that's holy, stop believing every "get rich quick" scheme that lands in your inbox.

74

We've become so used to instant gratification, we expect everything to happen immediately.

I remember a time before the internet, when waiting wasn't just a concept, it was a way of life. Need information? Hit the library and pray the Dewey Decimal System was on your side. Want to let your crush know you're into them? Better hope they catch that vague song request on Friday night's radio show. Now? We've got supercomputers in our pockets, and I can't even wait 37 seconds for my kid to put on her socks before asking Alexa about the weather.

This instant gratification culture is bleeding into our businesses, and it's jacking us up. We put out some social content and if we don't immediately get a flood of new followers or sign-ups, we think something's wrong. We pivot, we panic, we blame our offer. But here's the thing: real growth, meaningful success, it takes time. The magic happens in the consistency, in the daily watering and nurturing when you can't see a damn thing happening.

75

Just creating content for the sake of creating content is not going to solve anything. You need to create content that is designed to speak very specifically about who you are, what you offer, and why anyone should give a shit.

The online business world is drowning in a sea of bullshit content. Everyone and their dog is churning out reels, posts, and podcasts like there's no tomorrow. But most of it is about as useful as a screen door on a submarine.

I've seen it time and time again. Entrepreneurs frantically following content calendars, desperately trying to keep up with the latest trends. They're dancing on TikTok, sharing "vulnerable" posts on Instagram, and pumping out weekly newsletters. But for what?

Creating content just to tick a box is a waste of your fucking time. It's like shouting into the void and expecting the void to write you a check.

What you need is content that cuts through the noise. Content that grabs people by the collar and says, "Hey, listen up!" It's not about how much you put out there. It's about saying something that actually matters.

You've got to get crystal clear on who you are. Not the sanitized, people-pleasing version. The real you. The one with opinions, quirks, and maybe a potty mouth. Then, you need to nail down what you're offering. And I'm not talking about your "7-step program to whatever." I mean, what transformation are you actually providing?

But here's the million-dollar question—why should anyone give a rat's ass? That's what you need to communicate. In a world where everyone's vying for attention, you've got to give people a reason to stop scrolling and listen to you.

It's not easy. It's scary as hell to put yourself out there. But it's the only way to stand out in this overcrowded online space. So stop hiding behind generic content. Get specific. Get real. And for fuck's sake, give people a reason to care.

76

You will never go higher than the sum average of the groups that you are in, and that's a truth a lot of people do not want to hear.

I've seen it time and time again—people wondering why they're stuck, why they can't seem to break through to the next level. They invest in courses, hire coaches, and buy into every new trend, but nothing changes. The hard truth? It's often because of who they're surrounding themselves with.

Look, I get it. It's comfortable to stick with what you know, with the people who've always been there. But comfort is the enemy of growth.

I'm not saying you need to cut everyone off or join some exclusive club. What I will say is you need to be intentional with your energy and your attention. Your internal algorithm is always running, always seeking out more of what you feed it. So ask yourself: are you feeding it struggle and limitations, or possibilities and growth?

This isn't just about business—it's about life. The people you're following, the content you're listening to, the podcasts that you subscribe to, the kinds of conversations you're having, the kind of content you're engaging with—they all shape your reality. Be willing to outgrow spaces that no longer serve you. Because if you want to elevate, you need to be around people who are already there.

77

For when you're busy and you feel like you're getting things done, but you're on autopilot, nothing feels real and nothing feels enjoyable.

Twice a year I do a life audit. It's not some fancy, complicated process—it's just five questions that help me get my shit together when I feel like I'm going through the motions *(and not in a good way!)*.

First up, make a gratitude and celebration list. I'm talking about all the good stuff that's happened since January, or whatever timeframe you're looking at. And I mean everything—it doesn't matter how big or small they are. It doesn't have to be business related or income related. Just the good stuff, because our brains are wired to focus on the negative, and we need to hijack that.

Next, what I call loving truth bombs. This is where you look at what wasn't so great, what happened, or what transpired that you're like, "that was really hard," or, "I didn't like that," or, "I wish I didn't have to do that again." Then ask yourself, how many of those things were in my control? It's a huge reality check.

Third, check in on your goals. What were those resolutions or intentions you set at the start of the year? Do they still feel aligned? If not, give yourself permission to dump them and figure out what you'd rather do.

Fourth, evaluate your habits. What actions can you release that aren't serving you? What do you want to avoid or stop altogether moving forward? Then ask yourself, what's one small change that you can make over the next six months to get you closer to that?

Finally, the ditch list. This is where you ask yourself, who are you associated with or connected to that is bringing you down, that is making you feel overwhelmed or causing you to feel bad about your life and your business and your choices. Maybe it's time to mute or disconnect from some folks.

You can do this as often as you need. Maybe for you it is once a year or twice a year. Maybe it's quarterly. Maybe you need to do this every fucking week to begin with. That's totally fine. You get to decide.

When I sat down and worked through these five questions, holy hell, did things start to feel looser in my chest. It helped me clarify and remind myself what was important to me. Because that's one of the big truths we forget when we're feeling overwhelmed and stuck—it's usually because we've fallen off the path we truly desired for ourselves.

So give it a try. Take stock, get honest with yourself, and remember—you're not doing anything wrong. This is just part of the journey, and sometimes we need to pause and recalibrate. That's what this audit is all about.

78

You have to have the stomach for hard conversations. You have to be able and ready and willing to have these conversations. It's part and parcel of the gig.

I'm not just talking about the fun parts of running a business here. I'm talking about the nitty-gritty, the uncomfortable stuff that makes you want to crawl under your desk and hide. Yeah, that stuff.

Let me give you an example. A few months ago I had a situation. There was a client of mine who I have been with for nearly a year, suddenly drop me like a hot potato. No warning whatsoever, just a formal email 30 minutes before the end of the day. Talk about a punch to the gut.

Now, here's the thing. Could the client have done better? Abso-fucking-lutely. A face-to-face on Zoom, a quick huddle on Slack, hell, even a phone call would have been better than that cold, impersonal email. But you know what? That's not on them. That's on me.

Why? Because I should have created an environment where they felt comfortable having that hard conversation with me. I should have made it clear from day one that I can handle tough talks, that I'm not going to fall apart if they're not happy with something.

And let's be real here—these types of conversations are not easy to have. I get it. They're awkward, they're uncomfortable, and they make you feel like shit. But guess what? That's part of the gig.

When you decide to be a founder, a business owner, a CEO, or whatever the fuck you want to call yourself, you're signing up for more than just the glamorous parts. You're signing up for the hard stuff too. The stuff that keeps you up at night, the stuff that makes your stomach churn.

Avoiding these conversations doesn't make the situations go away. It just makes them bigger, uglier, and more painful when they finally explode in your face. Trust me, I've been there, and it ain't pretty.

Not to mention, every time you avoid that hard conversation, you chip away at your own integrity. You're telling yourself that your boundaries, your worth, your sanity are less important than keeping the peace.

So, what's the solution? Simple. Grow a pair *(and I don't care what genitalia you have, you know what I mean)*. Learn to have these conversations. Practice them. Get comfortable with being uncomfortable.

Start small if you need to. Tell your VA that their work isn't up to par, and how they can do better. Let your web designer know that the shade of blue they chose makes you want to gouge your eyes out. Whatever it is, just start having those conversations.

Because the more you do it, the easier it gets. And the easier it gets, the better you become at running your business. You'll build stronger relationships, you'll nip problems in the bud before they become catastrophes, and you'll sleep better at night knowing you're not avoiding shit.

79

Be happy to have people unsubscribe, because the more people that unsubscribe from your list, the closer you are getting to the right fit people.

When people unsubscribe, it's a good thing. It means you're getting closer to your true audience—the people who actually want to hear from you. Those are the people who will engage with your content, buy your stuff, and become your raving fans.

So stop freaking out about unsubscribes. Stop trying to inflate your numbers with shady tactics. Focus on creating valuable content for the people who want to be there. That's how you build a real, engaged audience. And trust me, that's worth way more than a bloated list of uninterested people.

80

Clarity is kindness, especially when it comes to things like feedback or advice or even matters of truth.

Let me tell you something that took me way too long to learn: being clear isn't being mean, it's being kind. I used to dance around issues, sugarcoat feedback, and wrap advice in so many layers of fluff that you'd need a machete to find the actual point. Why? Because I thought I was being nice.

Spoiler alert: I wasn't.

All I was doing was creating confusion and, honestly, wasting everyone's time—including my own. It's like trying to help someone navigate while giving them a map covered in unicorn stickers and glitter. Sure, it looks pretty, but good luck finding your way.

The real kindness? It's in the clarity. It's saying, "This project needs work" instead of "Oh, it's... interesting." It's offering specific, actionable advice instead of vague platitudes. It's telling the truth, even when it's not wrapped in a bow.

I remember the first time I gave clear, direct feedback to a team member. I was terrified. But you know what? They thanked me. Actually thanked me! Because for once, they knew exactly where they stood and what they needed to do next.

So here's my challenge to you: next time you need to give feedback, offer advice, or speak your truth, try clarity. Be kind. Be clear. Trust me, it's a game-changer. Your team, your clients, hell, even your family will thank you for it.

81

Sure, hire a VA, hire a support person. But is that the best first hire? I'm going to go out on a limb and say no, not always.

You're feeling overwhelmed, drowning in your to-do list, and some business coach tells you to just hire a VA. Problem solved, right? Wrong.

Hiring isn't a magic wand you can wave to fix your overwhelm. It's not as simple as "delegate that shit" and watch your business skyrocket. Let's get real for a second. If you don't have business coming in, what are you busy with on a day to day basis that you need to delegate?

Before you jump on the hiring bandwagon, take a hard look at what you're actually doing day-to-day. Are you busy with admin crap, or are you avoiding the scary stuff like putting yourself out there and selling?

Because let me tell you, a VA isn't going to magically bring in clients or refine your offer.

Sometimes, what you really need isn't a VA, but a kick in the ass from a coach or strategist to help you figure out what the fuck you're doing in the first place. Or maybe you just need someone to come in and clean your house so you can focus without distraction.

The point is, don't just follow the herd and hire because someone told you to. Be intentional, be honest with yourself, and for fuck's sake, figure out what you actually need first.

82

You're allowed to not do something just because you're good at it. I think if we could remember that, there would be a hell of a lot more happy entrepreneurs out there.

I've been there. Some well-meaning coach tells you, "Hey, you're good at it so you could make money doing it." And like the good little entrepreneur you are, you create an offer, try to sell it, and then wonder why you feel like you're dragging yourself through molasses every time you have to talk about it.

Being good at something doesn't mean you should monetize it. We're multifaceted creatures, capable of excelling at many things. But that doesn't mean we should turn every skill into a business offering.

When you create offers based solely on skill, without considering your purpose, your truth, what you want to do, you're setting yourself up for resentment and resistance. And then some guru will tell you it's a mindset problem or that you're shit at sales.

No, honey. It's not a you problem. It's a misaligned strategy problem.

So, take a breath. Sit down. And ask yourself: What do you want? Why? What does that look like from an action perspective? Your capacity, your daily focus, your long-term vision—these are the things that matter. Not just what you're capable of doing, but what lights you up.

Remember, you're building a business, not a prison. Choose wisely.

83

We are so anxious for everything to work out right away. We are all, myself included, impatient... and we make it harder than it needs to be.

We're all guilty of this shit. We launch our offer, talk about it a handful of times, and then freak the fuck out when we don't have a waitlist of clients banging down our virtual door.

But the reality is that building a business is like watching paint dry while riding a rollercoaster. Slow as hell, yet somehow terrifying.

We're so damn impatient, aren't we? I catch myself doing this all the time. I'll put something out there, and if I don't see immediate results, my brain goes into overdrive. "It's not working! Quick, burn it all down and start over!"

That impatience? It's what makes us overcomplicate everything. We throw handfuls of spaghetti at the wall, hoping something will stick, instead of giving our offers time to breathe and find their audience.

The next time you're tempted to scrap everything because it's not an overnight success, take a deep breath. Stick with it. Keep talking about your offer consistently for at least three months before you even think about pivoting.

Patience isn't just a virtue in business—it's a goddamn superpower.

84

What if most of us aren't actually introverts? What if the problem is that we have all been taught how to connect in a way that is actually just really shitty.

I've always thought of myself as an introvert. Socially awkward, shy, the person who needs time to recharge after social interactions. But what if that's not entirely true? What if our struggles with connection aren't about personality types, but about the way we've been taught to interact?

Think about it. Most of our networking events are just business card orgies. We're taught to approach people with an agenda, to see them as prospects or marks. It's all about what they can do for us, how they fit into our sales funnel. No wonder we feel drained and awkward!

But recently I attended a networking breakfast, and something just clicked. I didn't need downtime afterward. Why? Because for once, the connections felt genuine. We weren't trying to scratch each other's backs or grease palms. We were just...connecting. Talking. Being human.

Maybe we're not all introverts. Maybe we're just tired of shitty, transactional connections. What if we stopped trying to "network" and started trying to genuinely connect? No agenda, no elevator pitch, just real conversations. It might feel scary at first, but I bet it'd feel a hell of a lot better than another round of "What do you do?" followed by a business card exchange.

Let's try it. Let's be awkward, authentic humans together. Who knows? We might find out we're not as introverted as we thought.

85

Having a business is a responsibility, and it is your responsibility. There are some things that no matter how big you get, you can't really ever delegate.

Sure, you can delegate the day-to-day shit. But the core of your business? That's all you, baby. No matter how big you get, how many fancy titles you hand out, or how many zeros are in your bank account, you can't just check out and expect everything to run smoothly.

You're the visionary. You're the one who needs to be out there, carrying the vision, aligning with the mission, upholding the values. You also need to be selling your face, your service, your expertise. Because let's face it, your business is not just some faceless entity—it's an extension of yourself, your values, your dreams.

So yeah, go ahead and hire support. Delegate the admin crap that's bogging you down. But don't for a second think you can just step back and let someone else steer the ship. This is your journey, your vision, your responsibility.

Part 6

THERE'S NO SUCH THING AS ONE-SIZE-FITS-ALL

86

Success doesn't mean shit if it doesn't make you happy, and success is hugely subjective. You get to decide what success looks like, what it consists of, how it feels and what you're willing to do to achieve it.

Let's talk about the S-word, shall we? No, not that one—I'm talking about success. It's this shiny, elusive thing we're all chasing, right? But too often, we're running after someone else's version of it.

I mean, how many times have you seen those "How I Made Six Figures in Six Months" posts and felt like absolute crap? Or looked at Little Miss Perfect Entrepreneur with her color-coded planner and thought, "Damn, I must be doing something wrong"?

Success isn't a one-size-fits-all deal. It's not about hitting some arbitrary number in your bank account or having a bazillion followers on Instagram. Hell, it might not even be about your business at all.

Maybe success for you is having the freedom to pick up your kids from school every day. Or being able to take a nap in the middle of the afternoon without feeling guilty. Or hell, maybe it's making just enough money to support your fancy coffee habit and your dog's organic treat addiction.

The point is, YOU get to define what success looks like for you. And let me tell you, it's incredibly liberating when you finally give yourself permission to do that.

So, take a moment. Close your eyes. Imagine your perfect day. What does it look like? How does it feel? That, my friend, is your version of success. And don't let anyone—not your mom, not your business coach, and certainly not some rando on Instagram—tell you otherwise.

Remember, if you're not happy, what's the point? Life's too short to be chasing someone else's dream. So go out there and create your own definition of success. Make it weird, make it wonderful, make it uniquely you. Because at the end of the day, that's the only success that really matters.

87

I saw an ad the other day about how we should normalize making eight figures in business. Fuck you, that's all I'm going to say about that.

Actually, no. That's not all I'm going to say about that. Because this kind of bullshit is exactly what's wrong with the online business space. There are people out there right now who can't even make four figures a month consistently and you're over here telling me I got to make eight fucking figures a year?

This is the kind of toxic, unrealistic expectation that's burning people out and making them feel like failures. It's not just unhelpful; it's downright harmful. We're creating a space where anything less than astronomical success is seen as inadequate, and it's bullshit.

Success isn't about hitting some arbitrary number that someone else decided was impressive. It's about building a business that works for you, that aligns with your values, and that allows you to live the life you want. For some people, that might mean eight figures. For others, it might mean a comfortable five-figure income that lets them work from home and spend time with their kids.

We need to stop normalizing this relentless pursuit of more, more, more, and start normalizing contentment, balance, and businesses that actually serve the people running them—not just their bank accounts. So the next time you see an ad like that, remember: you're not failing if you're not making eight figures. You're just living in the real world, where success comes in all shapes and sizes.

88

There's no right way to do pretty much anything. There's only your way, and you get to tweak it and adjust it till it feels right for you.

The online business space is drowning in gurus spouting off about the "right" way or the "best" way to do things. I've lost count of how many times I've seen entrepreneurs tie themselves in knots trying to follow someone else's "foolproof" business strategy. But you know what? That's all bullshit. What works for one person might be a total disaster for another. Your business isn't just some cookie-cutter template—it's an extension of you, your values, and your vision.

So take all that advice with a grain of salt *(yes, even mine)*. Hell, take it with the whole damn salt shaker. Use it as a starting point, sure, but then make it your own. Tweak it, bend it, reshape it until it feels right for you.

And guess what? That "right" feeling might change over time, and that's okay too.

Remember, you're not on anyone else's timeline but your own. You're not stuck just because you're not hitting the same milestones as @BusinessBro69 on Instagram. You're on your own path, dancing to your own rhythm. So own it, adjust it, and keep moving forward. That's the only "right" way there is.

89

**You get to decide on your impact. The size and
the strength of it is entirely up to you.**

You did not come to entrepreneurship for shits and
giggles, right? There's a reason you're here, a mark you
want to leave on the world. And no matter what
anyone else tells you, only you get to define what that
impact looks like.

Now, I'm not talking about some grandiose, save-
the-world type of impact *(though if that's your jam, go for
it)*. Maybe your impact is spending more time with
your kids, or setting up trust funds for your niece and
nephew if you're the rich auntie type. Hell, maybe it's
just being able to donate to your favorite causes without having to worry about having enough to feed your
family.

The point is, you get to decide. Your impact doesn't have to look like anyone else's. It's not about conforming to some predefined notion of success or influence. It's about what you want to do with that money you're making *(because let's face it, that's the bare minimum. That's the ground floor reason why all of us are in business)*.

But here's where the magic happens. When you start speaking it out into the world, when you make it real and start talking about it like it's already happening—that's when shit gets interesting. You'll find your people. You'll create a community around it. You'll inspire others to tap into their own desired impact.

So, stop hiding behind vague mission statements or playing small. Share your vision with conviction. Because when you do, you're not just building a business. You're creating a legacy, your legacy.

90

There's a lot of magic in baby steps. We're all so focused these days on giant leaps, and I think that causes more problems than it alleviates, especially when you're not a long jumper.

Everywhere you look in the business world, it's all about "10x your growth" or "skyrocket your success overnight". Well, I'm calling bullshit on that noise.

Here's the thing: most of us aren't built for those massive, life-altering jumps. We're not all Elon Musk or whatever hotshot entrepreneur is trending on Twitter this week. And you know what? That's perfectly okay.

The real magic, the sustainable, soul-nourishing kind of progress, happens in those tiny, unsexy baby steps we take every day. It's showing up, doing the work, and inching forward, even when it feels like you're getting nowhere.

I've seen too many brilliant entrepreneurs burn out trying to keep up with some arbitrary timeline of success. They're so busy chasing after these massive goals that they miss the beauty of the journey, the lessons in the little wins and losses.

So here's my advice: ditch the pressure to make these grandiose leaps. Instead, focus on what you can do today, this week, this month. What's the next easiest step you can take? Do that.

Then do it again. And again.

Embrace the baby steps, celebrate the small victories, and watch as those tiny, consistent actions add up to something truly magical.

91

I don't want a seven figure business because I know what it would require for me to give up in order to maintain it.

Everyone and their dog in the online business space is chasing that seven-figure dream. It's like some magic number that supposedly proves you've "made it." But you know what? I call bullshit.

I've been there, done that, got the t-shirt. And let me tell you, the price tag on that t-shirt? It's steep as fuck. It cost me my kids' firsts—first steps, first words. It cost me my sanity, my presence, my ability to just be a mom without feeling guilty.

So yeah, I don't want a seven-figure business. And I'll keep saying it until I'm blue in the face. Because I know exactly what I'd have to sacrifice to get there and maintain it. And frankly? It's not worth it. Not to me.

My definition of success? It's being able to drop everything at 2:30 PM to pick up my kids. It's having the freedom to say "fuck no" to early morning calls. It's being present, really present, not just physically there while my mind's off running numbers.

Don't get me wrong. If a seven-figure business aligns with your why, go for it. But don't chase it just because some guru told you that's what success looks like.

92

Are you doing things in your life or your business because you're more concerned with how it looks than how you feel?

We've all been there, right? Doing things because we think we're supposed to, because that's what some guru said, or because we're afraid of how it might look if we don't.

We're taught to push through, to hustle, to scale at all costs. But here's the thing: You get to lean into what feels right or feels good, or feels easy. You get to do or not do things just because that's how you feel.

It's not about being flaky or unprofessional. It's about having success without the BS. It's about building a business that honors you, your life, and your vision. Because when you're doing something that doesn't feel right, you won't do the best job you absolutely can at it.

So, I invite you to take a step back. Look at your life, your business. Where are you feeling that resistance? What feels heavy? It's okay to acknowledge it. It's okay to change course. Let it be okay, and then decide what the fuck you want to do about it. Because at the end of the day, your business should bring you joy, not just look good on paper.

93

If you are breaking even every month, you are successful. If you are making enough money to cover all your expenses and you're not going into debt, you are successful.

Success is not about hitting arbitrary numbers or achieving X, Y, Z in the first 30 days. That's just a quick way to set yourself up to feel like a failure.

If you're breaking even every month, you're successful. If you're making enough to cover all your expenses and you're not putting yourself in debt, you're successful. Full stop.

This isn't about settling for less. It's about setting monetary targets that are actually meaningful.

I know, I know, it's not sexy. It's not going to get you on the cover of Forbes. But you know what? It's the foundation of a sustainable business.

94

When you focus on everything that you haven't accomplished, it takes all of the focus off the enormous amount you have accomplished.

You know what's fucked up? How easily we forget our wins. We're so busy chasing the next big thing, we don't stop to appreciate how far we've come. And I'm as guilty of this as anyone.

Every year, as Q4 rolled around, I'd get caught up in this frenzy of "oh shit, look at all this crap I didn't do." I'd beat myself up over arbitrary goals I hadn't hit, completely overlooking the incredible stuff I had achieved. It's like we're all programmed to focus on the negative.

That's why I started my weekly wins journal. Every Friday, I write down all the great things that happened that week. It's not always easy, especially when life's throwing curveballs at you left and right. But it's a game-changer.

Now, when I'm having a bad day, I flip through that journal. It's like a highlight reel of my year, reminding me of all the awesome shit I've done. It's my personal "fuck you" to the Q4 push and all that FOMO-inducing bullshit.

So take a moment to celebrate your wins, no matter how small. Because at the end of the day, that's what really matters. Not some arbitrary goal you set back in January, but the actual progress you've made. Trust me, you've done more than you think.

95

You can have success without all the fucking BS that they keep telling us is normal, but it has to start with questioning the status quo.

I've been in this game long enough to smell bullshit from a mile away. And let me tell you, the stench of "all in" rhetoric is overpowering. We've been fed this lie that success only comes to those who sacrifice every-thing—their time, their health, their relationships—on the altar of business.

I've seen it time and time again. Entrepreneurs burning themselves out, employees getting chewed up and spit out by corporations demanding their souls. And for what? A pat on the back and a "good job" from some CEO who can't even remember your name?

You can build a kickass business, have a thriving career, and still have a fucking life. Novel concept, right? But it starts with calling out the BS. It's about looking at these "normal" expectations and saying, "Nah, I'm good."

Success isn't about being "all in"—it's about being smart, strategic, and true to yourself. It's about setting boundaries, prioritizing what matters, and telling the hustle culture to go fuck itself. Because at the end of the day, if your success costs you everything else, is it really success?

So here's my challenge to you: Question everything. Push back. Redefine success on your own terms. Because trust me, there's a better way—and it starts with you refusing to swallow the BS they're serving.

96

You are worthy simply because you exist. You don't have to keep putting things on your list to prove your worth.

I want you to take a good, hard look at that to-do list of yours. Go on, I'll wait.

Now, tell me honestly: how many of those items are there because you genuinely want or need to do them? And how many are there because you think they make you a "good" person, a "successful" entrepreneur, or a "worthy" human being?

I'll bet you my favorite pair of yoga pants that at least half of that list is just you trying to prove your worth to the world. And honey, you've got nothing to prove.

You don't need to earn your place in this world. You're not some corporate cog that needs to justify its existence through endless productivity. You're a living, breathing, magnificent human being. And that alone makes you worthy.

I know, I know. It's a hard pill to swallow in a world that's constantly telling us we need to do more, be more, achieve more. But think about it: did you have to earn your right to breathe? To exist? Hell no! You came into this world worthy, and nothing—not your bank account, not your follower count, not your perfectly color-coded planner—can change that.

So, the next time you're about to add another "should" to your list, pause. Ask yourself: "Does this matter right now?" If it's not truly important to you, cross that sucker off.

Remember, you get to decide what success looks like, what it consists of, how it feels and what you're willing to do to achieve it. And if that means having a shorter to-do list and a longer nap time, then so be it.

You are worthy simply because you exist. Full stop. Now go take a nap, you magnificent creature.

97

I'm not here to build a business of clout or have that #LaptopLife, because even the rhetoric of time freedom and money freedom and location freedom is superficial.

The online business space is drowning in bullshit promises of freedom. Time freedom, money freedom, location freedom—we're told to aspire to this because it's supposedly the beauty of being an entrepreneur. But honestly? It's just another shiny distraction from what really matters.

Think about it. How much money is actually "enough" for freedom? Is it the magical eight-figure mark everyone's touting now? Funny how that used to be seven figures, and before that, six.

Here's a reality check: most entrepreneurs never even hit six figures. That's the cold, hard truth.

And time freedom? Don't get me started. We're all chasing this mythical four-hour work week. But is that even possible? Or desirable? The truth is, most of us are working more hours than we ever did in our corporate jobs.

As for location freedom—have you seen the state of the world lately? Travel is expensive as fuck, airlines are a shitshow, and oh yeah, the climate crisis means everything's on fucking fire.

Chasing these so-called freedoms is just keeping us stuck in the same rat race we were trying to escape. It's time to wake up and realize that true freedom isn't about hitting arbitrary benchmarks or living some curated Instagram life. It's about building a business that actually aligns with who we are and what we want—not what some guru tells us we should want.

98

Know what the fuck you're getting into. Know what it takes and what you have to give up or gain in order to make it work.

There's a ton of bullshit out there about what it means to be successful in business. Everyone's trying to sell you on their version of the dream—scale up, build an empire, be the next big thing. But bigger isn't always better and smaller isn't for everyone.

You want to scale? Cool. But understand what that really means. It's not just about growth. It's about strategically growing the business to keep up with market demand while improving efficiency and increasing profit margins. Sounds great, right? But it comes with a price.

As you scale, you might find yourself keeping certain clients you're not jazzed about just to pay your team. You'll be doing double and triple time on marketing to feed the machine. And that whole "I'm still the boss. I get to make the decisions in the business" thing? Yeah, that starts to change when you've got a leadership team to consider.

On the flip side, staying small as a solopreneur? It's not a cop-out. It's a valid choice. You get more flexibility, higher profit margins, and the freedom to pivot without upsetting a whole team's apple cart.

The bottom line? There's no one-size-fits-all in this game. Your version of success might look different from the next entrepreneur's, and that's perfectly fucking fine. Just make sure you know what you're signing up for. Do your homework. Understand the trade-offs. And for the love of all things holy, don't let anyone tell you you're doing it wrong just because you're not chasing their definition of success.

Your business, your rules. Just make sure those rules are based on reality, not some hyped-up fantasy of what entrepreneurship should look like.

99

Success has less to do with how long and how hard you work and way more to do with having the capacity, emotionally, mentally, spiritually, physically, to play the long game.

We've been fed this narrative that success is all about grinding, hustling, and burning the midnight oil. But here's the thing: success is not a quick win and it's not about how many hours you can clock in before you collapse.

I used to be that person, you know? I was that employee that just worked until they pretty much fell over. And guess what? It didn't make me successful. It made me a burnt out, resentful mess, and ultimately, it's why I left my corporate job.

Here's what I've learned since becoming an entrepreneur: Success is in the longevity that allows you to truly set up the life you desire and continue enjoying what you do more days than not. It's in having the stamina to keep going, to keep innovating, to keep serving your clients or customers year after year.

And you know what gives you that stamina? It's not working 80-hour weeks. It's having the capacity, emotionally, mentally, spiritually, physically, to play the long game. It's about taking care of yourself so you can show up fully for your business and your life.

So, how do we do this? We start by deciding what's important to you. Maybe it's health, family, fitness, or even sleeping in late. It doesn't matter. That it's important to you is what matters.

Then, we create boundaries to protect these priorities. We honor what is important to us.

Remember, you get to decide each day what you have the capacity for and what you don't, and you get to plan around that. Some days, you might work longer hours because you're in the flow. Other days, you might need to step back and recharge. And that's okay. That's not failure, that's sustainable success.

So, let's redefine success. Let's make it less about the hours logged and more about the life lived. Because at the end of the day, isn't that why we became entrepreneurs in the first place? To reclaim the autonomy, the choice of how we want to fill our days. That, my friends, is true success.

100

There is absolutely nothing wrong with staying a solopreneur or running a lean business.

This idea that you're somehow failing if you're not scaling your business to the moon? It's bullshit.

I'm a solopreneur. I've been a solopreneur from the very start. And you know what? I fucking love it. I do sometimes hire contractors on a project basis when I need support in certain areas, but otherwise, it's just me, myself, and I running this show. And guess what? I take home a lot more of my income than some of my counterparts who have larger businesses with bigger expenses and overheads, and I'm not working nearly as hard or as long as people think.

Lower overhead, higher profit margins—that's the solopreneur sweet spot.

Sure, some gurus will tell you that your income is capped because you, as a business owner, only have so many hours in the day. But what they don't tell you is even when you scale, your income is still capped because your team only has so many hours in a day. And now you still have to pay the team.

As a solopreneur, I can pivot, I can change my target audience and my ideal client much more quickly than if I had a bigger-scaled business. I don't have to keep working with certain clients because I need the income to pay my team. I get to decide who I work with, what I offer, and how I price it.

So if you're happy being small and lean, own it. Don't let anyone make you feel like you're doing business wrong just because you're not chasing their version of success. Your business, your rules. And if those rules involve keeping things small and mighty? More power to you.

WANT MORE BUSINESS BLASPHEMY?

If you've made it this far, you're clearly ready to challenge the status quo and build a business that actually works for you. But why stop here?

Join me every week on the *Business Blasphemy* podcast, where we continue to question the sacred truths of the online business space and uncover what it really takes to build a business that honors your life and vision.

You'll get more no-nonsense insights, hard truths (with a side of excellent puns), and occasional curse words as we navigate the BS of entrepreneurship together.

Listen wherever you get your podcasts.

ABOUT THE AUTHOR

Sarah Khan is the fiery founder of Corporate Rehab® Strategic Consulting, a boutique business advisory firm.

From managing multimillion dollar corporate projects to launching her own successful online consultancy, she taps into 20 years of experience to craft clear and direct paths to success for her clients.

In her role as a Leadership Architect and Identity Strategist, she works with women leaders and entrepreneurs in professional services to craft unignorable personal leadership brands as the foundation for impact, influence and income by design—whether that comes from starting their own business, writing a book, commanding bigger stages, snagging coveted consulting contracts, or more.

Connect with Sarah:

    in @sarahikhan

    f @the.sarah.khan

    @corporate.rehab

    www.GetCorporateRehab.com